GOLF
explained

HOW
TO TAKE ADVANTAGE
OF THE RULES

By PETER DOBEREINER

Illustrated by
Bert Kitchen

*For John and Robert, who saw what golf
did for their father and took to other games.*

©1977 by Peter Dobereiner

Originally published in Great Britain under the title "Stroke, Hole or Match?"
©1976 by Peter Dobereiner. Rules of Golf ©1976 by the Royal and Ancient Golf
Club of St. Andrews. Illustrations by Bert Kitchen ©1976 by David & Charles
(Publishers) Limited.

Manufactured in the United States of America

Published in 1977 in the United States of America by Sterling Publishing Co., Inc.,
419 Park Avenue South, New York, N.Y. 10016

Library of Congress Catalog Card No.: 76-51177
Sterling ISBN 0-8069-4110-3 Trade
                    4111-1 Library

CONTENTS

ACKNOWLEDGMENTS

When I asked Gerald Micklem if he would read the manuscript of this book and check it for technical accuracy he readily agreed, greatly encouraged me by his enthusiasm and made many valuable suggestions. Without his expert help I would never have dared to go to publication and I thus gratefully add myself to the long list of people in all walks of golf who have benefited from his profound knowledge of the game and his generosity.

I am also grateful to the Royal and Ancient Golf Club for permission to reprint the Rules of Golf from the 1976 edition published by the Royal Insurance Company, and I must emphasise the interpretations of them in this book are entirely my own and the Royal and Ancient bear no responsibility.

INTRODUCTION

Hardly a week passes without a new book on golf coming off the presses somewhere in the world. Millions of words about the game pour forth in different languages. They tell us how to play the game, about the history of golf and describe the personalities of the great players. The author of yet another golf book, therefore, bears a heavy responsibility for adding to the verbal cataract. So allow me to mount the penitent's stool and make a personal plea in justification of this book.

To be frank, I did not want to write it; I would much prefer that someone else had written it thirty years ago. That would have saved me much grief and anguish. But nobody did write it and so when I began to play golf I had only the haziest idea of the rudiments of the rules of golf. Some lucky beginners are weaned on golf, growing up under the guidance of fathers and friends wise in the ways of this absorbing game.

My apprenticeship was totally erratic. Like many golfers I picked up my knowledge of the rules in haphazard fashion like a bird scavenging for crumbs. Scraps of information – and misinformation – came my way and embarrassing experiences filled in some of the gaps. I still blush at the memory of holing a long putt only to have my elation turn sour at the caustic response of my opponent that I had lost the hole for striking the flagstick. Losing the hole was bad enough but being exposed as a golfing ignoramus was even worse.

The painful episode haunted me for weeks. It seemed so unfair. After all, there was no logic in it. What difference did it make if you putted with the flagstick in the hole? You could never make a shrewd guess, based on natural sporting instincts and common sense, that it would be wrong to hit the flagstick. I thought it all very unfair (and, as a matter of fact, I am still far from happy about that particular rule of which the only purpose it seems to me is to make the game slower).

Anyway, while my enthusiasm for golf grew, my respect for the rules remained dormant, to say the least. In due course I became professionally involved in golf as an author and journalist and had to absorb the rules as thoroughly as I could.

My hang-up about the wisdom of rules, or some of them, persisted and I delighted in writing articles in newspapers and magazines railing against the complexities and apparent anomalies of golf law. Basically, I reasoned, golf is a simple game – in the procedure, you understand, not the execution, which has always eluded me – and it requires only a few simple rules. The earliest surviving code, the articles of the Honourable Company of Edinburgh Golfers, 1744, had only thirteen rules and the last of these was really a special local rule: *Neither Trench, Ditch, nor Dyke made for the preservation of the Links, nor the Scholars' holes, nor the Soldiers' lines, shall be accounted a Hazard, but the Ball is to be taken out and Teed, and played with any iron Club.*

If our forefathers could get along happily enough on the iron rations of a dozen basic rules, why do we need fifteen paragraphs on etiquette, thirty-five definitions, forty-one rules with clauses, subclauses and appendices as numerous as the grains of sand in Hell bunker? And that is just the basic skeleton of golf law. In addition it is fleshed out with fat volumes of case law in the form of decisions which have been handed down by the Rules of Golf Committee on appeal.

The moment of my deepest disenchantment with this unwieldy structure of legalistic rigmarole came during the Ryder Cup match at St Louis in 1971 between the United States and Great Britain and Ireland. In the four-ball series of the second day, Arnold Palmer and Gardner Dickinson were playing against Bernard Gallacher and Peter Oosterhuis. The Americans had the honour on the par-3 7th hole. The caddies for the match were college students who were naturally enough delighted at the opportunity to spend a week in the company of their heroes.

For them it was the chance of a lifetime. No one except a churl could blame Gallacher's student caddie for excitedly asking Palmer what club he had used for his towering shot to the green 208 yards distant. 'Heck! It looked to be only a mid-iron.' Palmer replied, 'Five-iron.' Gallacher did not hear this whispered exchange at the side of the tee because by now he was addressing his ball. But the referee heard it and instantly recognised a breach of the rule which forbids the asking of advice from anyone except your own partner or either of your own caddies. The referee conferred with two distinguished and learned committeemen and after the hole had been completed as a half in 3s, the referee gave his decision: the British pair had lost the hole. Naturally the incident caused considerable embarrassment all round, not least to Palmer himself, and there was much comment from members of both teams along the lines that such a purely technical infringement would have been better dismissed by an attack of diplomatic deafness on the part of the referee.

I felt no outrage at the decision but was appalled at the treasure hunt through the rule book which was needed to track down the decision. A whole series of points had to be established. Was Gallacher responsible for the action of his caddie? Did the caddie's question: 'Great shot! What club did you hit?' constitute the seeking of advice under the meaning of the definition? If so, it being a four-ball, was Gallacher only to be penalised or did any penalty apply to Oosterhuis as well? And finally, what was the appropriate penalty – loss of hole or disqualification? Hours later, after much private conferring in committee with deep research into the law books, an official statement was issued tracing the legal process through two definitions and three rules of golf. As a matter of incidental interest I had done a personal search through the rules and after a number of re-starts from false clues I had arrived at the conclusion that the British pair should not have lost the hole. The correct ruling, by my researches, was disqualification. That experience brought home to me more strongly than ever a guilty realisation of my ignorance of the rules. And that was just silly. Here I was, paid to write about golf and interpret it for my readers and I could not honestly say that I knew the rules of the game. Actually that was not quite as absurd as it may sound because very few people are fully conversant with every ramification of every rule. Every year we find examples of men who have played golf professionally all their lives who accidentally infringe a rule through ignorance.

Anyway, from the time of that Ryder Cup ruling I decided that since I could not influence the lawmakers to simplify the rules, I would just have to buckle down and make a thorough study of those 35 definitions and 41 rules and all those confusing sub-clauses. My first conclusion came as a great surprise. After years of complaining about the excess of verbosity in the rules, I discovered that they were written with the greatest economy. How often I had scoffed at the superfluity of paragraph 7 in the preamble to the rules. *Every word means what it says.* In fact, that is an important point to bear in mind when reading the rules, which are absolutely precise. And while they may have about them the arid and stilted style of all legal literature, they also possess a certain elegance. The trouble about them, of course, is that being set out in legal style, using words such as 'hazard' where we golfers commonly talk of 'bunker' or 'trap', the lay mind finds them difficult to absorb.

For most of us, accustomed to reading books and newspapers and absorbing the general sense of what is written without paying close attention to precise detail, there is not much difference, for example, between the expression 'a club' and 'the club'. To the golf lawyer there is a vital distinction and that tiny difference can involve a penalty. Rule 19, for example, says that the ball *must be fairly struck at with the head of the club and must not be pushed, scraped or spooned.* There was an appeal to the Rules of Golf Committee from a player whose ball had lodged firmly in a pine tree. The tree was so thick that the player felt it was useless to try to dislodge it with one club. He therefore grasped a bundle of three clubs and smashed into the tree with this battery of ironmongery. The ball popped out on to the green but the player was penalised for using three clubs. He appealed against that ruling on the grounds that he did not honestly believe he had made contact with the ball with one club, let alone three of them. The Committee upheld the penalty decision because of that word 'the'. 'The club' can only mean one club and so Rule 19 had been infringed.

The one rule which survives in the essential sense from that earliest Edinburgh code reads: *He whose Ball lyes farthest from the Hole is obliged to play first.* I once felt that the lawmakers should have retained that wording if only as a reminder of golf's ancient origins. After all, its says everything a golfer needs to know. But does it? The modern rule (20) reads: *When the balls are in play, the ball farther from the hole shall be played first. If the balls are equidistant from the hole, the option of playing first shall be decided by lot.* Grudgingly I have to admit that the modern version is more precise, even if only because it gives tacit recognition to women golfers by eliminating 'He' and by making provision for the equidistant situation.

It was this problem of legalistic interpretation which convinced me that a book would be useful if it could present the rules in simple, everyday terms in such a way as to make them understandable and memorable. Hopefully, the illustrations will help that purpose. In no sense is this book intended to be a substitute for the official version. My aim has been to provide an introduction to the main rules (I have omitted some of the more esoteric ones such as the technical specifications for clubs and balls) so that the beginner will have a grounding in the laws and will be able to refer to the official rules when necessary with the confidence of knowledge. At the same time I have tried to distil and explain the philosophy behind the rules since it is always easier to act correctly if you understand and respect the reason for the things you are required to do. I hope that such explanations will reduce some of the undoubted sources of confusion. For instance, there is a rule (9) which includes the provision that you must not have a mark placed on the line of your shot (such as parking a caddie car on the skyline for a blind shot) or have anyone stand close to the line while you play the stroke.

In a tournament in England a player called a penalty on another competitor because the caddie held up the flagstick to indicate the line of a blind shot to the hole. In fact, there should have been no penalty because another rule (34) specifically permits the flagstick to be held up to indicate the position of the hole, regardless of where the player may be. That incident, which unhappily resulted in a player being wrongfully disqualified, also illustrates another side of the rules. Most people see rules – and indeed laws of all kinds – as a series of prohibitions carrying penalties for the transgressor. Woe betide us if we break the law. But the rules should not be seen solely as a list of 'Thou shalt not' commandments. They also incorporate the golfer's Bill of Rights and that is another good reason for knowing them thoroughly. The case histories of golf are full of tragic examples of players who have lost important competitions simply because they were not sure of their rights. There is nothing unsporting about using the rules to your advantage wherever possible. Indeed, it can happen that if you sportingly decline an opportunity to take your due advantage, then you actually become liable to a penalty. A famous example occurred at the British Open Championship at Troon in 1973. Tony Jacklin's ball landed in a rabbit hole and under the provisions of Rule 32 he dropped the ball without penalty two club-lengths clear. On hitting the ground the ball rolled a few feet further from the rabbit hole and into a much better lie. Jacklin did not know his rights in this case. (The rules permit a dropped ball to roll a *further* two club-lengths, making four club-lengths in all, from its original position so long as it does not finish nearer the hole.) Jacklin felt that this lucky roll was giving him an undue advantage and in a spirit of fair play he picked up his ball to drop it again. His action was seen and he was duly penalised for touching his ball when it was in play. Quite possibly Jacklin's good intentions and instincts for fair play on that occasion cost him the championship.

The lesson must be to play to the letter of the law, accepting its bounties as well as its penalties, with equal grace. The laws, which are administered by the Rules of Golf Committees of the Royal and Ancient Golf Club of St Andrews and the United States Golf Association, and jointly revised every four years, try to be fair. But no rule can legislate for every case which may arise in a game played over such a diversity of country as a golf course. For every golfer there will be occasions when the application of a rule will appear totally unjust or absurdly benevolent.

Accept them both, according to the letter of the law. But there will also be times so unusual that no rule of golf covers the situation. Then you can safely give rein to your sense of fair play and natural justice. The rules say so. They call it equity. Use it sparingly even in social golf games with your friends. In the long run both you and your friends will get more satisfaction from your golf if you meticulously adhere to the rules. And by cultivating the habit of being a stickler for the rules you will greatly reduce the danger of embarrassment or disappointment when you come to play in serious competition.

NOTE: Where there is a number in parentheses after a heading or elsewhere in the text, it refers to the rule being discussed. The full rules are to be found beginning on page 132. A glossary of golf terms begins on page 125.

1 ON THE TEE

Know your own ball — Learn the rules — Fourteen clubs — The teeing ground — Ball falling off tee-peg — The honour — Stroke and distance — Rule 1 — Stroke- and match-play

KNOW YOUR OWN BALL (21)

Before starting a round of golf you have an important responsibility — to make sure that you can identify your ball. As we shall presently see, there are severe penalties for playing a wrong ball. Even the wide variety of manufacturers' markings are inadequate to guarantee that two players in a four-ball are not using balls of the same brand and number. Most professionals add a distinctive personal mark with the point of a pencil, such as dotting the 'o' of 'Dunlop', to eliminate any possibility of later confusion. There is no need for the ordinary club player to go to these lengths. All that is necessary is for you to tell the other players in your group the brand and number of your ball. Then any duplicate can be exchanged before you hit off. However, if you run low on ammunition and have to play a similar ball to one someone else of your group is using, give it a distinguishing mark.

On the subject of ball markings it might be worth mentioning a useful convention in the event of a lost ball. If you hit into heavy rough and opponents or fellow competitors join you to look for it, as hopefully they will, it is a good idea to repeat the brand number as you begin the search. That policy eliminates any possibility of friction arising from someone finding a ball and asking 'What were you playing?' It is a natural enough question to ask but it can be misinterpreted as a cross-examination to guarantee that you do not claim a ball that was not yours. As if you would! So start the hunt by shouting 'I'm playing a Slazenger 6' and then if any other ball is found it can safely be picked up by the finder without suspicion or embarrassment.

LEARN THE RULES (37)

A further important preliminary to a game of golf is to familiarise yourself with any local rules, which should be printed on the score card or posted on the club notice board. You will get no sympathy by complaining that you did not realise that a certain path was out of bounds. The rules emphasise the responsibility of the golfer to familiarise himself with the laws of the game and the special local rules and, as in the larger game of life, ignorance of the law is never acceptable as an excuse. In any case it is only sensible to read the local rules. It has happened to every golfer that during a round he gets into trouble, consults the back of the card and then moans: 'If I'd known it was out of bounds over here I'd never have played that shot.' Local rules, like the other rules, can help a player as well as hinder him. In this game we need all the help we can get, so take a minute or two to absorb the local rules.

FOURTEEN CLUBS (3)
Another duty before teeing off is to check that you do not have more than fourteen clubs with you. That is the legal limit and this is an appropriate point to introduce one of the basic philosophies on which the whole structure of golfing law is based. Despite what the frustrated golfer might imagine as he grapples with the complexities of the official code of rules, with its myriad clauses and sub clauses, the rules basically derive from common sense. When a golfer is unsure of a rule, he should ask himself the question: 'What is the fair and logical thing for me to do in this situation?' On most occasions the answer suggested by common sense will be correct under the laws. Take this fourteen club rule. You are out playing and you accidentally break a club. Can you replace it? Yes, you can, common sense tells you, because you will still be within the fourteen club limit. And that is what the rule says. (Mind you, that does not mean you can run back to the club from the far end of the course to fetch a replacement from your locker. Then you would be infringing the rule against playing without undue delay. (37–7) But common sense tells you that, too.)

The same logic suggests that *deliberately* breaking a club, such as snapping your putter across your knee in a fit of pique, is a different kettle of fish entirely. That's nobody's fault but your own and, just as common sense makes it obvious that after such temper tantrums clubs cannot be replaced, so do the rules of golf.

It is equally obvious that if you start with fewer than fourteen clubs you can make up the number during the round. Less obvious, so mark it well, is

If you deliberately break a club, say in a fit of pique, then you will have to complete the round without it for it may not be replaced .

that you cannot replace a club or make up your quota of fourteen by borrowing from anyone who is playing on the course. If borrowing were allowed, two partners could carry twenty-eight different clubs between them and exchange at will, thus making a mockery of the fourteen club limit. Partners are allowed to share clubs only when they have a maximum of fourteen between the two of them.

There is one practical complication about the fourteen club rule. Manufacturers normally make clubs in sets of four woods, eight or nine irons, wedge, sand-wedge and putter. A so-called full set of sixteen is therefore illegal. In theory, the golfer who owns such a beautiful quiver of clubs is supposed to take notice of such factors as the weather and the state of the course, and then discard those clubs he thinks will be of least use to him. But all too often he omits that ritual and discovers on the first tee that there are 15 or 16 clubs in his bag. Must he now drag all the way back to the club-house or his car to discard the unwanted ones and keep his companions kicking their heels on the tee, possibly missing their place in the starting time? No. The rules permit him to declare specified clubs to be out of play. They can then stay in the bag provided, of course, he does not use them. If so, he is disqualified. By the same token, a player who discovers an extra club during the round and takes his penalty can declare that club out of play.

Penalty scale for carrying more than fourteen clubs
Penalties for carrying excess clubs, *regardless of the number of extra clubs in the bag*, are as follows:

Match-play: loss of each hole on which the violation occurred with a maximum penalty per round of loss of two holes.

Stroke-play: two penalty strokes on each hole on which the violation occurred, with a maximum penalty of four strokes.

Stableford: deduct two points from the final tally for each hole on which a violation occurred, with a maximum penalty deduction of four points.

THE TEEING GROUND
With those preliminaries out of the way, we are now ready to go on to the tee, which is the area of prepared ground at the beginning of each hole. We are concerned with that part of the tee called the teeing ground, a rectangle

extending back two club-lengths from a line between the markers. (The rules of golf make frequent mention of this measurement of 'two club-lengths'. By all means measure off with the longest club in your bag and take fullest advantage of this wording when it suits your purpose.) The ball must be teed-up within the rectangle although you may stand outside it if you wish (13). For instance, if the area is particularly worn you may well want to tee the ball at the extreme backward limit of the teeing ground and in that case your right foot would be outside the teeing ground. But beware of teeing-up too far forward. We all need every inch of advantage or think we do, and it is very easy on occasion to tee-up in front of the markers, especially if they are not set exactly square to the line of shot. Now we may be in trouble unless some kindly soul points out the error before the ball is hit.

In stroke-play if you hit off from outside the teeing ground, you have to count that stroke and then play another from inside the proper area, using a tee-peg again if you like. If you fail to rectify your mistake you will not have played the stipulated course and will be disqualified.

In match-play your opponent can recall a shot played from outside the teeing ground and make you play again. In that case there is no penalty. The humiliation is punishment enough without making you count that first, foul shot.

BALL FALLING OFF TEE-PEG (14)
Having teed up your ball in the right place, it commonly happens that the ball falls off the tee-peg or is knocked off it by the club-head at address. Well, the answer to that one is usually that some comedian calls out: 'One!' The Rules of Golf Committee has so far failed to devise a suitable penalty for those guilty of perpetrating the oldest joke in golf, so that player's only redress in the matter is to shrivel the wretch with a telling response. As for the ball, it can be replaced on its tee with no penalty. However, if you have actually started your downswing when the ball topples from its tee, that is just too bad. You have made a stroke within the meaning of the laws and must count it, whether you make contact with the ball or not. Further, by your act of making a shot you have put the ball into play (even though you may have missed it). So in that case you cannot replace the ball on its tee-peg. By touching a ball in play, except in accordance with a specific rule, you would become liable to a two-stroke penalty (or loss of hole in match-play).

THE HONOUR (12)

With our clubs duly counted and the identity of the ball established, the round can begin. Who is going to hit first? This is called taking the honour and although it is seldom of any great practical consequence, it is a distinctive part of golfing ritual and an important reminder that golf is an honourable game based on sportsmanship. In organised competitions, the players hit off the 1st tee in the order in which they appear in the draw. If there is no official list, then the honour is decided by lot, in the legal terminology. In other words, you toss a coin for it. But most golf is played socially at club level and in this case there is a long established convention for the player with the lowest handicap to hit first. Equal handicaps toss for it.

A note of caution must be sounded at this point. That convention about the lower handicap man playing the first shot in friendly games is one of several customs which have grown up in golf but which are at variance with the rules. What difference does it make, you ask? None at all! It is only a harmless and generous gesture of respect towards the superior skill of the better players. If the law condemns it then the law is an ass! If we want to play it that way, who is to stop us? The answer is that nobody will stop you. The custodians of the laws of golf are not in the slightest degree interested in how golfers behave in their private games of purely social golf. But if you habitually give the low-handicap player the honour in private matches, it is quite possible that you will automatically follow the same practice in an official competition, such as a club medal tournament.

Now the whole legal apparatus of golfing officialdom does become involved because the first rule of the tournament will be (or certainly should be) *The competition will be conducted under the Rules of Golf as approved by the Royal and Ancient Golf Club of St Andrews and the United States Golf Association.* Any query will be referred to one of these two bodies for arbitration. And they, you may be sure, will have no truck with any excuses such as 'But we always do it like that at our club.' The law says the honour shall be decided by lot and that's that.

It is no use pointing out that there is no penalty for playing out of turn in stroke play. That applies only in taking the honour by mistake. If you have tacitly conspired with your fellow competitor to ignore the rule and follow the usual convention, then you are automatically guilty of a breach of Rule 4 which forbids, under penalty of disqualification, any agreement to waive a rule. You could be ordered to give back a prize. The sensible thing, surely, is to bury the convention about low-handicap men hitting off first and get into the habit of tossing a coin. That settles the question of who hits first. From then on the honour goes to the player with the lowest score on the previous hole. If the hole is completed with the same scores, the honour does not change. In match-play, if you mistakenly steal the honour by playing out of turn off the tee, your opponent can demand that you abandon that ball and play another in your proper turn. There is no penalty other than the embarrassment, just as in the case of playing from outside the teeing-ground. There is no power of recall in stroke-play and no penalty. The ball is in play right enough but stealing the honour is an act of discourtesy and if committed deliberately the committee of a competition could impose a general penalty.

STROKE AND DISTANCE

There are not very many more ways you can fall foul of the law on the tee, and you may feel there are just about enough since you have not yet struck a ball, but the possibilities which remain are of the highest importance and should be thoroughly absorbed. They cover the procedure for lost ball, out of bounds or ball unplayable, and these rules, which apply right through the game, form the very foundation of golf law. We will examine them in detail later. For the present let us concentrate on one of golf's earliest precepts. From the time men first began to play golf, whenever that was and wherever it may have been, they held to the principle that the ball must be played as it lies (16).

We can tell from the specialised clubs, such as rut irons and water-mashies, how reluctant our forefathers were to deviate from that cardinal brief. We must still honour that central concept of playing the ball as it lies. That ought to be an article of faith for every golfer even though the rules nowadays permit many deviations from the original ideal. But right from the start men ran into predicaments which made it impossible to continue the game without some form of escape clause. After all, if your ball was lost in a lake, you had to do something about it. So came into being the stroke-and-distance rule. Down the centuries golfers have scratched their heads and asked 'What do I do about that?' and their opponents have answered 'Stroke and distance.'

So let us get this stroke-and-distance rule firmly established because that is the principle from which many variations in golf law flow. If your ball is lost, or out of bounds, or is stuck up a tree or, as once happened, has fallen down the chimney of a greenkeeper's cottage and plopped into a pan of stew simmering on the hob, you can invoke the stroke-and-distance rule. You may go back to the place from which you hit the last shot (in this case you are still on the tee), play another ball and add one penalty stroke to your score. Stroke and distance is the blanket rule which covers all occasions – your next shot off the tee is your third. If you play another ball from the tee under the stroke-and-distance rule you are at liberty to tee-up the ball again.

RULE 1

As we replace the head covers on our drivers and walk up the fairway, let us reflect on some of the other basic precepts of this absorbing game of golf. Take Rule 1 which simply says: *The game of golf consists in playing a ball from the teeing ground into the hole by successive strokes in accordance with the rules. Penalty for breach of rule: match-play – loss of hole; stroke-play – disqualification!* What does it mean? On the face of it the rule appears so obvious as to be unnecessary. Taking the component parts of the rule separately it can be made to sound so banal as to be absurd. *Playing a ball* – well, what else? . . . *from teeing ground into the hole* – well, no one would try it the other way round . . . *in accordance with the rules* – so you have to obey the rules; there's a novelty! In fact, Rule 1 serves an important purpose because even some of those obvious provisions can be broken. Golfers have frequently missed their way on strange courses and holed out on, say, the seventh green thinking it to be the sixth. Rule 1 covers that situation.

In another case, on a course where two holes had teeing grounds of successive holes next to each other, some players hit tee shots from both tees to save themselves the labour of walking back the length of the first of the two holes. That practice was ruled contrary to Rule 1 because they did not complete the round in successive strokes. But Rule 1's most important purpose is to give competition committees blanket powers to deal with irregularities. Most rules carry their own individual scale of punishments which are laid down to cover accidental infringements. But serious or deliberate offences – let us not be mealy-mouthed about it, that means cheating – clearly need to be punished more severely, and in such cases Rule 1 can be invoked.

Perhaps a brief note on the morality of golf is in order at this point. It is very easy to cheat at golf. Probably no other game offers more scope to unscrupulous players who are willing to take advantage of the fact that they are often hundreds of yards away from any witness. The ball can often be nudged up on to a friendly tuffet during the address with no risk of detection. In the rough the lie can be improved in many clandestine ways. One of golf's jokes concerns a foursome match (in which partners take alternate shots at the same ball). One player hit into dreadful jungle and his partner disappeared into the undergrowth where he was heard thrashing about wildly. 'Is it playable?' shouted the first golfer and received the classic reply 'Not yet.' That story may or may not strike you as funny but in real life cheating is not amusing. It happens, of course, even at the highest level and scandals rock the game from time to time. But golf is a game of trust and the vast majority of players treat it as such.

That does not mean that golfers as a breed are necessarily more honest than other people. It simply reflects the fact that golf is a diversion. It is meant to give the player pleasure. And while golfers find different pleasures and satisfactions in the game according to their natures, there is precious little sense of accomplishment to be had from returning a good score or winning a match by cheating. In this respect golf is like solitaire. No one stops you cheating at solitaire but what fun is there in 'getting out' if you manipulate the cards to gain that end? The exercise loses its point and so it is with golf.

STROKE- AND MATCH-PLAY

Everyone who is interested in golf enough to have read this far will know that there are two forms of the game – stroke-play (counting the total number of shots for a round) and match-play (played by holes). The rules for these two forms of the game vary slightly, as we have already seen in the matter of playing out of turn on the tee. Various studies have been made from time to time with the object of simplifying the rules so that the same code and the same scale of penalties could apply for both stroke- and match-play. One anomaly in the dual system, for example, is that the general penalty in stroke-play is two shots and loss of hole in match-play (5). Now for a first-class golfer who can be expected to play 18 holes in 72 shots the stroke-play penalty is 1/36th part of a round while the loss of hole penalty is double, 1/18th part. For humbler players the discrepancy is even more marked. All attempts at unifying the rules have so far foundered – on the rock of tradition rather than because of insuperable legal problems, many of us feel – so for the moment there is nothing else for it but to learn both sets of rules. As if the poor beginner did not have difficulty enough in mastering one lot! In practice there are not too many pitfalls in the dual code. The majority of the rules apply to both forms of golf and circumstances will normally dictate when and how the match-play variations should be applied.

The one danger to avoid is to try and play both forms simultaneously. If you are playing a match do not say to your opponent: 'If you don't mind I'll mark a card as well for handicapping purposes.' When you proudly report your victory to the competition secretary he is likely to award the match to your opponent – and reject your card for handicap adjustment as well. The reason for this ban on what might appear to be a harmless, indeed convenient, practice is that there are significant variations in the rules for the two forms of golf which make it impractical to play both forms simultaneously.

2 THROUGH THE GREEN

Advice and assistance — No mark on line — No improving of lie or line — Practice strokes and swings — Foreign materials — Artificial aids — Ball unfit for play — Cleaning the ball

Golf is a lonely game. In spite of its associations with conviviality and sociable club life, it is essentially a highly introverted pastime. At every level of the game the golfer is on his own the moment he steps up to address his ball. His friends are silent (or so we hope) and retreat from the golfer's consciousness. Now it is just him, a club and a ball. In theory there ought to be no great difficulty about hitting the ball. It requires no great physical strength to swing a club weighing less than a pound — although we may think it needs all the exertion we can produce. The action of swinging a club is not complicated or difficult — although most of us make it so. And the degree of precision needed to implant the club-face flush to the ball is no greater than a hundred everyday actions which we unerringly perform without conscious thought. If you swat a sitting fly and knock the head off a daisy with a walking stick, then you can play golf.

If we could play golf with the same conditioned instincts we would have no problem. But we cannot. The fact is that golf is difficult because we make it so. All manner of inhibitions and fears rise up in the mind of a man about to hit a golf ball, some of them demons of his own creation and some impressed on to his imagination by the daunting sight of the way ahead.

There is nothing like an expanse of water, for instance, to produce an involuntary tightening of the hands on the grip and a resolve to give this one a little bit of extra effort. And then, usually in combination with an irresistible urge to look up and see the result of the shot, the golfer is lost. What was basically a straightforward pitch shot has turned into a feverish ordeal entirely through the interaction of past memories, self-doubts and visual forebodings in the mind of the golfer.

So the golfer is really playing against himself. He is his own enemy far more than any flesh and blood opponent. Golf is therefore much more than a test of manual skill and dexterity. It is also a trial of character and the rules reflect this aspect of the game. We have already touched on one element of this side of golf in discussing the heavy degree of trust which golf lays on the honesty of the player.

ADVICE AND ASSISTANCE (9)

The loneliness of the golfer is further emphasised by the ban on receiving advice and assistance. The rule says you must ask or receive advice only from your partner or either of your caddies. Advice is defined as any suggestion which could influence you in making up your mind about how to play, what club to use or what type of shot to attempt. Information about rules or local rules is specifically exempted from the rule, so although the answer to a question such as 'Is it out of bounds over that fence?' might well influence you in planning your shot, it is allowable. But 'What club did you hit?' as we saw in the case of Bernard Gallacher in the 1971 Ryder Cup match, is construed as asking for advice. It has also been ruled that asking if the flagstick is on the back or front of the green does not constitute seeking advice since it is public information and simply saves the player walking forward to see for himself.

Similarly, you can ask anyone the line of play, such as 'Is this a dog-leg to the right?' Another seemingly mad part of the rule prohibits you from seeking physical assistance in making a stroke, such as having a friend steady your trembling hands on the putter and guiding the club for you, or from accepting protection from the elements. So do not allow your caddie to hold an umbrella over you when you are making a stroke.

It is in this area of pernickety regulations that the rules of golf could possibly be simplified. That ban on physical assistance, plus rule 19 about forbidding the ball to be pushed, scraped or spooned and a few others are so outlandish and obvious that they could surely be incorporated into one blanket rule requiring that the game be played in accordance with established custom and tradition.

NO MARK ON LINE (9)

The final part of the advice-and-assistance rule is one of the least known (or least observed) laws of golf. It says that through the green you may have the line of play indicated to you by anyone but no mark must be placed on the line and no one may stand on or near the line while you play the shot. This rule is frequently broken on undulating courses which involve blind shots. A player walks uphill to survey the way ahead, parks his bag or caddie car on the skyline and then returns to his ball, carrying the selected club. The shot is then played directly over the mark on the skyline, often in ignorance of the rule but illegally for all that. A two stroke penalty or loss of hole should be imposed.

This is the rule *through the green* and is superseded by the laws covering the green itself. You can have the flagstick held up to indicate the position of the hole at any time, whether you are on the green or not.

One innocent trap awaits the unwary in this prohibition about putting a mark on the line. In their instruction books, many great players such as Jack Nicklaus advocate picking a mark, such as a daisy, just in front of the ball and then hitting over that mark. That is fine. But if there is no suitable mark on your intended line you might be tempted to pick a daisy and place it in front of the ball. And that would never do.

NO IMPROVING OF LIE OR LINE (17)

By now the precept of playing the ball as it lies will be well understood. That thought can be extended to the wider principle that the golfer must accept the consequence of his previous shot. If you are in trouble then you have to play out of that trouble as you find it. We will come to the exception to that precept — such as an unplayable lie, impediments and obstructions — in another chapter but for the moment we will stay with situations which, however unpleasant, are free of such complications. The rule says that you must not improve the lie of your ball or the line of the shot or the area of your swing *by moving, bending or breaking anything fixed or growing, or by removing or pressing down sand, loose soil, cut turf placed in position or other irregularities of surface which could in any way affect your lie.* Obviously, if your ball is in a thicket you could not get to it without *bending anything growing* so the rule provides specific exceptions. These are:

> *In fairly taking your stance;*
> *In making the stroke;*

When teeing the ball;
In repairing damage to the green.

Let us look at those four exceptions with some care because this is another rule much abused by golfers at all levels.

In fairly taking your stance. The important word here is 'fairly' and you must be the judge of that. If your ball is in bushes you must clearly bend growing branches when you take your stance. What you must not do is wield your wedge like a machette and hack away inconvenient vegetation. Nor must you pull aside branches and trap them under your foot because that is not fairly taking a stance. You must not trample behind the ball, flattening the undergrowth for a clean shot at the ball. This is a favourite dodge of the golfing cheat. He positions his bag in such a way that when he addresses the ball and then changes his mind about the choice of club, his foot naturally comes down behind the ball as he steps across to make a new selection. After a few such changes of mind he can confidently get a straight-faced club to what had previously been a hopeless lie.

A variation on this ploy is to stand beside the ball idly making practice swings in the pretence of total absorption in the difficulties of the shot but in reality hacking away inconvenient tuffets or saplings.

In the case of saplings and young trees, these are sometimes staked and provision is made in the local rules for a free drop clear of them. Wilful destruction of growing vegetation has no place in golf. Rather than risk demolishing a young tree or shrub a thoughtful golfer will accept the penalty of declaring his ball unplayable (of which more later).

That injunction, which has nothing to do with the rules of golf, applies equally to the second exception, *in making the stroke.* When you swing the club you may well break or bend growing vegetation and provided it does not constitute the kind of vandalism mentioned above, that is perfectly all right.

The third exception, *when teeing the ball*, means in practice that you are free to tread firmly behind your teed ball to press down loose earth or grass. And the fourth exception, *on the green*, covers the repair of pitch-marks, of which more anon. Having absorbed the intention behind this rule, it ought to be easy enough to remember two further provisions. You must not build a stance, such as by scraping up loose sand to create a level area; your only entitlement is to place your feet firmly (which includes a degree of shuffling and squirming). And if your ball is in long grass, or similar concealing conditions, you can only touch as much of it as to enable you to find and identify your ball. You must in no way improve its lie and the rules insist that you have no divine right to a sight of your ball as you play the shot.

There has been one decision on the rules for improving the line of play which illuminates the philosophy underlying these regulations. A player whose ball was off the green wanted to use his putter but there was a puddle of water on the green in the line of his shot. He wanted a free drop to a position which would give him a water-free line to the hole but this request was quite properly refused because his ball was not on the green. The player therefore had his caddie mop up the puddle. The Rules of Golf Committee decreed that this was unlawful action to influence the movement of a ball.

PRACTICE STROKES AND SWINGS (8)

Some of the most straightforward rules cause the most trouble. Take the example of Rule 8 which simply states: *During the play of a hole, a player shall not play any practice stroke.* Remember that a *stroke* is defined as the forward movement of a club with the intention of hitting the ball. What could be easier to understand and remember? The reason for the rule is apparent; golf would be a much easier game if we could all play practice strokes and then, once we had found the best way of playing the shot by trial and error, we could say: 'O.K. This one is for real.' That would not be golf and the fact is so obvious that the rule is almost superfluous. This is not one of the rules which is wired into the golfer's mental alarm system because such hypersensitive precautions are not necessary. And there lies the danger. For instance, a competitor in a national amateur championship found an old ball in the rough. It had been badly chewed by a dog, or fox, and was therefore absolutely useless for any purpose. Even the most impoverished enthusiast would have rejected it as a gift for his practice bag. The player remarked to his fellow competitor: 'There is only one fate fit for this miserable specimen' and idly chipped it into a lake. Most of us have done the same sort of thing from time to time in social games. But this was a serious competition and the golfer was guilty of playing a practice stroke. He was duly penalised two strokes (in match play he would have lost the hole).

This is a good example of how the rules must be applied literally, without regard for the most innocent of intentions. So if you are held up on the course and must expend your restless energy on swinging a club, make sure you do not use a ball. It is perfectly all right to make practice swings, swishing at daisies or thrashing the empty air, or even hitting acorns and chestnuts. And if you are making a practice swing on the tee and, as sometimes happens, you smack the club into the turf with such violence that the seismic vibrations dislodge your ball from its tee-peg, that does not count as a stroke since you had no intention to hit the ball. But until you have completed the hole be sure not to hit practice strokes of any kind. Once you have holed out, and before starting to play the next hole, you are allowed to while away the time (always provided you are not holding up play) by replaying putts on the green you have just completed or trying to chip into the trash basket by the next tee, or play practice shots provided you avoid two punishable offences: you must *not* make a practice stroke out of any hazard and you must *not* play a practice stroke on – or on to – any green except the one you have just completed. The usual penalties apply – two strokes or loss of hole (the *next* hole, that is not the one just completed).

Of course, there is an obligation on every golfer to show due consideration in this business of practice shots and practice swings. It is inexcusable to gouge divots out of the tee, or indeed the surrounds, as you swing away waiting for your opportunity to start play at the next hole. Incidentally, you should not replace divots on the tee, the one occasion when the bleeding wound in the turf should be left open. And it is equally uncouth to play practice shots which might disturb another player. Championships have been lost by players inadvertently taking practice strokes, notably the New Zealand Open Championship of 1937. A former winner, A. Murray, was waiting for a fellow competitor to putt out before he himself could complete the hole and he absent-mindedly dropped his ball at the edge of the green and played a practice putt.

FOREIGN MATERIALS (2)
James Braid, the great Scottish champion, who ruled the roost of British golf for many years in company with Harry Vardon and J. H. Taylor as 'The Great Triumvirate', always carried a piece of chalk in his golf jacket. He advocated that in wet weather the face of the driver should be rubbed with

chalk to dry the surface and give a better purchase on the ball to impart back-spin. That was a common dodge among the professionals of the day but latterly the Rules of Golf Committee have clamped down on the addition of 'foreign material' to either ball or club during play for the purpose of changing their playing characteristics. So much for the wonder aerosol sprays which advertisers tell us will add yards to the flight of a golf ball. Even if true, such foreign material would be illegal. (You can *clean* clubs and ball, of course, because this is not intended to change their playing characteristics.)

That sounds like a straightforward rule, but it had one tragicomic consequence for the English tournament player, Guy Hunt, a smallish man who needs all the help he can get to achieve distance off the tee. He discovered that when his driver was wet it put less backspin on the ball, just as Braid had explained. But Hunt was not interested in backspin, which is what gives the ball a high, floating trajectory. He wanted distance and with a wet-faced driver his shots flew lower and, with more run, farther. He therefore fell into the habit of licking his thumb and wiping it over the face of his driver. It was Lee Trevino, the American multiple champion, who first alerted Hunt to the dangers of this practice. Hunt was thoroughly embarrassed at the thought that he might have been infringing a rule of golf and his form suffered badly. He wrote to the Royal and Ancient Golf Club at St Andrews for a ruling. Meanwhile Hunt experimented with different drivers and adjustments to his swing to improve his driving with a dry-faced club. In due course the R and A exonerated Hunt but later had second thoughts and decreed that spit on the driver was a foreign material added to change the club's playing characteristics. Fortunately, by now Hunt had returned to form and was driving well with his new spit-free method, so the decision did not bother him. That is a way-out example but if you are of an experimental turn of mind, you might, for instance, be tempted to add a piece of lead tape to your driver. If so, do not do it during a round because that most definitely would come under the heading of changing the character of the club during play.

ARTIFICIAL AIDS (37)
In the same spirit, the rules try to maintain the natural feeling of golf by banning artificial aids (under penalty of disqualification) such as range-finders, wind gauges and spirit levels for measuring the slopes on the green (all of which have been marketed from time to time). If you want to judge

the speed and direction of the wind you are allowed to hold up a handkerchief or toss a few blades of grass into the air. As for judging distances you may well ask about those yardage charts which the professionals prepare for tournaments and which are increasingly available commercially for many courses. Well, the rules obviously permit their use although you should not dally too long pouring over your notes and pacing off from your markers. This could be held to be unduly delaying play.

People who need glasses are not infringing the rule against artificial aids but it is interesting to speculate on the subject. Glasses are normally made up for long sight or close work, or are combined as bifocals. Opticians can just as easily make up glasses focused on the exact distance between the eye in the address position and the ball. Such glasses are invaluable to players who naturally see an indistinct image of the ball they are addressing since the eye is the key to the whole series of reflex actions involved in the swing. Would such golf glasses, useless for any other purposes, be classified as an artificial device? It is impossible to anticipate the answer since no test case has yet been put to the Rules of Golf committees. On the one hand they seem to qualify as an artificial device under the rule but they also do no more than put the wearer on a par with normally sighted players. So they give no special advantage. All they do is enable a man with failing faculties to continue playing the game – but so did croquet putting, now outlawed (35). We shall have to wait and see the outcome of that one. Hand-warmers are legal, provided golfers use them to warm their hands and not their golf balls.

BALL UNFIT FOR PLAY (28)

It is appropriate before leaving the subject of defective sight to cover one possible result of such infirmity, namely damage to that expensive golf ball. If your ball becomes so badly damaged that it is unfit for play, you may substitute another during play of the hole where the damage occurred and in the presence of your opponent or marker. That means that if you cut your ball on the second hole, you cannot suddenly decide to change it halfway up the fifth fairway. (You can change your ball at any time between holes, of course.) This is one of the rare occasions when you *place* a ball during play through the green instead of dropping. The idea is to give yourself the identical lie. Mud sticking to your ball is patently not damage in this sense and cannot be said to have made the ball unfit to play. That is just bad luck. Can it be cleaned in any circumstances? Let us see.

CLEANING THE BALL

Very few golfers are totally confident about their rights in this business of when the ball may be cleaned. Some clean the ball every time they pick it up and often enough they get away with it because their opponents are not sure enough of their ground to exact the penalty. Others have a vague idea that cleaning is forbidden in some circumstances but, not being sure which these illegal instances might be, they never clean the ball and thus deny themselves a quite legitimate advantage. It is not a particularly important point in everyday, social golf but when competition days come around every golfer should make it a point of honour, not to say common sense, to observe every rule to the strict letter. After all, some of us can reflect ruefully on the day when we played and scored well, only to be denied a prize because of penalty strokes. It is only through such hard experiences that many golfers become aware of the more esoteric rules.

There are two occasions when you are allowed to clean your ball. The first is when you are *on the green* before each putt (35), although this right is thoroughly overdone and once should be enough on most occasions. Excessive ball cleaning is one of the main causes of slow play. The second occasion is *when you are taking relief* – that is to say, when lifting from an unplayable lie (23); when lifting from an obstruction; when lifting from ground under repair, burrowing animal scrapes or casual water; and when lifting from a water hazard.

It follows that you are *not* allowed to clean when lifting your ball to identify it, except by the minimum amount necessary to make the identification, when you have to mark and lift your ball through the green because it is interfering with someone else's stroke; and when you are replacing a ball which has been moved by an outside agency.

Perhaps it will help to clarify the rule to remember that if you are picking up your ball for any reason, you can clean it if you are putting it back into play in a different position; you cannot clean (except on the green) if replacing it in its original position.

The convention among professionals when they have to lift a ball on a cleaning-forbidden occasion is to pick it up between two extended fingers and then to hold it up rather ostentatiously to show that they are not doing a bit of unobtrusive rubbing with the thumb. Such flaunting of holiness may appear slightly rich for ordinary occasions, but at least it is preferable to an accusation of sneaking a surreptitious clean.

A word of caution is in order at this point on the method you use to restore your ball's pristine condition. By far the commonest practice is a quick lick and wipe of the ball on a towel, or, more likely, your shirt. This is not to be recommended because strictly speaking it is unlawful. Human saliva has been ruled to be a 'foreign material', although there is no recorded instance of a penalty being imposed for licking. More to the point, some highly toxic chemicals are used by greenkeepers, especially in control of worms so licking golf balls can cause severe belly ache.

It may be asked why you should be allowed to clean your ball on one occasion and not on another. Some people go so far as to advocate that golfers should be permitted to clean a ball at any time, since mud on the ball makes it impossible to exercise full control over the shot. It would seem, therefore, that the rules favour the luck of the bounce rather than skill. That is exactly the case. In a cross-country game such as golf, the element of luck can never be eliminated entirely. The luck of the bounce, enshrined in the expression 'a rub of the green', has always been an integral part of golf and one of the functions of the modern custodians of the game's traditions is to retain the spirit of the game as best they may.

Over the years concessions have been grudgingly made about cleaning the ball but only to the extent of easing situations in which golf becomes unplayable. It sometimes happens, for instance, that when you play from a particularly glutinous lie the ball sticks to the club face. It has been ruled in that case that the rule of equity operates. You pick the ball off the club face and drop it, without penalty, as near as possible to its original lie. Then you have another go, but you do not clean the ball in the meantime. You are stuck with the mud, and vice versa.

But you could have elected to declare your ball unplayable in the first place. If you had done so you would have had to pay for it, and the lawmakers, in their infinite charity, have decreed that a wipe of the ball is part of the bargain for your payment of a penalty stroke. Golf offers many dilemmas as to which option you should most prudently select and part of the skill of the game lies in making a wise choice.

Having made provision to clean the ball in taking relief from an unplayable ball, it is a matter of consistency to allow cleaning when obtaining relief for other reasons, whether free or under penalty. As for cleaning on the green, often a ball arrives on the putting surface in a totally unputtable condition. For a time there was a rule that you could clean your ball once only on the green but that legislation was rescinded, and now you can clean on the green as often as you like.

3 PENALTIES

Two stroke penalties — One stroke penalties — Unplayable lie —
Ball out of bounds — Boundaries — Lost ball — Provisional ball —
Alternative ball — Ball moved — Identifying ball — Wrong ball —
Bunkers and water hazards

TWO STROKE PENALTIES

Before examining the troublesome situations in which a golfer may find himself, let us look at the philosophy of golf penalties. Many golfers are confused over the scale of penalties and even after years of experience they are still unsure about which situations call for a two stroke penalty and those which carry only one stoke. Generally speaking, the two shot penalty, or loss of hole in match-play, is the punishment for a player accidentally breaking a rule of golf. (Deliberate breaking of rules, or cheating, is always punishable by disqualification.) So all those mishaps like playing a wrong ball, or shanking and hitting your own golf bag with your ball, or having your putt hit the flagstick, incur the standard two stroke penalty.

ONE STROKE PENALTIES

One stroke penalties are not really punishments. They are in two categories, the first of which we might think of in terms of prices. For example, if your ball is in a bush you have to decide whether to have a hack at it or whether it is worth the price of declaring it unplayable and dropping clear. In that case you are exercising your right to lift and drop at the cost of one stroke. In effect, you are buying your way out of trouble. The same principle applies to the case of having your ball land in casual water in a bunker. You have to ask yourself whether to take a free drop in the bunker or whether it is a worthwhile bargain to 'spend' a penalty stroke on the right to drop the ball outside the hazard. The other class of one stroke penalties are 'ghost' strokes. The rules of golf say in effect that if your ball is moved accidentally, perhaps as you were picking up a loose twig, then that is the same as if you had moved it with a club. So that's a stroke. In the same way, an air shot is a ghost stroke, in its effect on the ball. But you intended to hit the ball and must count the stroke. Another common ghost stroke is when you address the ball and it moves as you ground the club. Now we have to be absolutely precise at this point. It is quite common for the ball to move slightly when it is addressed, notably with a putter, and it is up to the conscience of the golfer to identify the type of movement. If the ball simply rocks slightly and settles back in exactly its original position, then no penalty is involved. But if the ball moves, if only by a fraction, and comes to rest in a new position, then the rules (27) say that is one penalty stroke, except when addressing the ball on the tee.

It often happens that a ball sitting in the rough will move when addressed by a club; the act of placing the club-head by the ball disturbs the grass and the ball is dislodged. That is why many professionals and good amateurs make a point of never grounding their clubs in the rough. By keeping the club-head clear of the grass, they do not risk accidentally causing the ball to move. What is more, if the ball should happen to move anyway, perhaps through the spontaneous collapse of supporting grasses, they are still in the clear because technically they are not at the address. Under the rules, a player is in the address position when he has taken his stance and has grounded the club behind the ball. (In a hazard you are at the address position as soon as you take up your stance because you are not allowed to ground your club in hazards.)

UNPLAYABLE LIE (29)

Many golfers look on the rules as a series of prohibitions and penalties set to trap them and punish their innocent mistakes. In fact, the rules can be allies as well as enemies and one of the most important examples of the rules as the golfer's Bill of Rights is the unplayable lie concession. We have already seen how the principle of the ghost stroke works.

If you accidentally move your ball, such as by inadvertently kicking it during a search or starting it to roll by moving a dead twig, then the rules say, in effect, that this is the same as if you had moved the ball with a club and you therefore add a penalty shot to your score (27). Now the same principle is extended to allow you to do the same thing deliberately by 'paying' a stroke. The first thing to remember is that it is your decision to declare your ball unplayable. It can be in a perfect lie in the centre of the fairway if you like. It is up to you and no one can question your right to declare your ball unplayable at any time, or in any place (except in a water hazard) even on the green. In practice, of course, you use this device only when your ball is in a fairly desperate situation and you feel it to be a bargain to extricate it at the cost of a stroke.

If you do decide to declare your ball unplayable there are three courses you can follow for the price of your penalty stroke. First, you can follow the stroke-and-distance procedure by going back to the spot from which you played the previous shot. If that happened to be a tee shot, then you are at liberty to tee-up your ball again. Otherwise you drop the ball or, if on the green, you place it.

The second option is to drop the ball within two club-lengths but not nearer the hole. The ball can now roll another two club-lengths quite legitimately without needing to be re-dropped. Indeed, you would incur a penalty if you picked it up, because it is now in play.

Great care should always be taken when dropping a ball because it can happen that having paid your penalty and taken an unplayable ball drop, the ball can roll into more trouble. The Rules of Golf Committee was asked to give a decision on the case of a player who declared his ball unplayable and took a drop only to have the ball roll against a tree trunk. It was within the limit of two club-lengths and not nearer the hole. He felt that he should get another drop, without penalty, as he had already paid to get relief from an unplayable lie. Not at all, ruled the wise men. The player had three options under the unplayable ball rule and having taken the risk of the two club-lengths process, he must face the consequences. Therefore he must either play the ball as it lay against the tree or declare it unplayable again with another penalty stroke.

The third action you can take is drop the ball as far as you like behind the spot where you declared it unplayable, keeping that spot between you and the hole.

It is extremely important to be clear on that last point as it is one of the most abused procedures in golf. One of the commonest situations for invoking the unplayable lie rule occurs when you hit into trees at the side of the fairway and your ball ends up against a tree trunk or in a bush. In that case many golfers who are not thoroughly conversant with the rule and simply have a hazy notion that you can drop as far back along the line as you like, assume that this means the line along which the ball entered the woods. They therefore go back towards the tee, or towards the spot where they played the last shot, and drop the ball as soon as they are in the clear. That is quite wrong. If you are in woods such as those we have been discussing, then the correct procedure – keeping the point of the unplayable lie between you and the hole – would take you deeper into the woods. So get the provisions of this rule absolutely clear in your mind and save yourself the embarrassment of being accused of trying to take unfair advantage. The rules try to be fair and the golfer who tries to follow that same precept of fairness will not go far wrong. On that basis it should be easy enough to remember that if you declare your ball unplayable in a bunker, then you must drop it in the bunker.

Now let us look at some unusual situations where the unplayable ball rules can be used. What if your ball gets stuck up a tree? Well, Arnold Palmer had that problem in Australia and he chose to climb the tree and play the ball, which he did with remarkable success. But that kind of adventurous behaviour is not recommended. In climbing the tree you might dislodge the ball (penalty stroke) and if it fell against the tree trunk, you would have to declare it unplayable (another penalty stroke). Better to declare it unplayable before touching the tree. Now you can dislodge it in any way you like. But, you say, what if the ball was more than two club-lengths above the ground – how could it be dropped? That problem has been covered by the legislators; you measure your two club-lengths from the point directly below where your ball lodged in the tree.

An appeal was once made over the case of a player who climbed a tree. His weight caused considerable movement of the trunk in which his ball was lodged but it remained securely wedged in a fork. The question now arose whether he was guilty of moving his ball. Although the ball was clearly in motion, the committee decided that no penalty was called for since the ball did not move in relation to its surroundings.

BALL OUT OF BOUNDS (29)

If you clearly see your ball go out of bounds then the procedure is simple. You apply the stroke-and-distance rule by going back to the place from which you played the last shot. You are already rooted to the spot in all probability, hopping from foot to foot and cursing your bad luck. You drop another ball (tee it up if on the tee) and add a penalty stroke. That means in the case of a drive, of course, that your next tee shot will be your third stroke. In common golfing parlance this is called hitting three off the tee.

BOUNDARIES

The difficulties arise when you are not sure if your ball is out of bounds. It is the club's duty to define its boundaries and explicit details should be provided with the local rules on the back of the score card. But problems do arise in borderline cases and one of them should be noted because it is at variance with what you might expect from your knowledge of common law. Where fences are used to mark a boundary, it is common practice to string the fence wire, or nail the runners, on the outside limit of the property, or the far side of the posts. In golf the boundary is always the line drawn between the inside limits of the posts and you are out of bounds when all of your ball is over that line. Thus there is a strip of no man's land the thickness of the posts which is out of bounds for golfers but nevertheless is within the boundaries of the club. If a trench is used to define out of bounds, as along the top of the famous Cops of Royal Liverpool, the trench itself is out of bounds. And when a line is drawn to mark the boundary, the line is out of bounds. But there is nothing to stop you standing out of bounds to play a ball which is in bounds.

LOST BALL (29)

Now the matter becomes slightly complicated, but so long as we keep the principle of stroke and distance in mind, then it will make the alternative procedures all the easier to remember. You see your ball disappear from sight into an area where there is a good chance it will be lost. Forget about water hazards for the moment, which are governed by a special procedure which will be explained later. For the present let us stick with the other manifold opportunities for losing a ball. If you see it heading for an area where you think it may be lost, here is what you do. You either formally abandon it and put another ball into play or you announce that you propose to play a provisional ball and, if on the tee, you tee up another ball and hit it, after everyone else has driven off. If necessary, you go on playing that provisional ball until you reach the area where you think your original may be. Now, on arrival at the search area, there are two things to be done: announce clearly to everyone helping in the hunt the brand and number of your ball; and take note of the time. You are allowed five minutes to hunt for a ball and at this point you wave through any players who are waiting behind (def 6).

This business of calling through players behind you is one of the most important courtesies in golf and sadly it is becoming more and more neglected. There are few greater frustrations than to be held up during a round while the players in front search for a ball. If your ball cannot be found within the five-minute limit then it is officially lost and you continue the hole playing your provisional ball under the stroke-and-distance rule. That is to say, you count the original shot from which the first ball was lost, plus one penalty stroke and all the strokes played with the provisional ball. If the original ball is found you play on with it, and simply pick up your provisional ball, without penalty.

PROVISIONAL BALL (30)
This use of a provisional ball is simply a device to save time: it is intended that if you have to apply the stroke-and-distance rule you do not have the bother of walking all the way back. Of course there will be many times when you have no advance inkling that your ball will be lost. You have driven off and walk forward confidently but when you get up there you can see no sign of the ball. You call the match behind through and search for five minutes without success. Now you have no option but to go back to where you played the last shot and play under the stroke-and-distance rule. There is absolutely no way of avoiding that long walk back, which can be highly embarrassing on a crowded course, and so it is a good idea always to play a provisional ball if there is the slightest chance that your original ball may be lost. After all, it does not cost anything in the way of penalties to play a provisional ball and you get more golf for your money.

ALTERNATIVE BALL
There is another occasion on which the playing of another ball can be used to save time and argument and wear on the nervous system. If a knotty point of golf law should arise (and even if you learn this book by heart there will be occasions when you are unsure how to proceed) you may find yourself at

odds with your companions. Someone will perhaps say that you can have a free drop but you yourself, by now hopefully a firm devotee to the play-it-as-it-lies principle, will be unsure that this suggestion is firmly founded on the rules. After all, there are very few golfers who are thoroughly familiar with every nuance of every rule although many are prepared to put forward their misguided judgements with confidence. For instance, it may be felt that your ball is in a place which is possibly ground under repair, or affected by an obstruction, or borderline casual water. If there is any doubt, follow both courses of action (11). Play the original ball as it lies and take his suggestion by dropping an alternate ball as well in the place suggested by the doubtful rule. Play out the hole with both balls and when you complete the round put the problem to the committee for a ruling before you sign your card. If the committee rules that the alternative ball was put into play in accordance with the rules the score with the alternative ball shall count. You can only use this alternative ball procedure in stroke-play. (In a match every dispute must be settled on the hole where it occurs.) And before you put an alternative ball into play you must declare your intention to do so to your marker or companions. (See page 87.)

Before moving on from the problem of lost ball, we should examine some of the difficulties we may meet during the actual five-minute search. One possibility is that you may take one horrified look at the area into which you saw your ball disappear and decide that it is hopeless even to begin looking for it. In that case you can abandon the ball but a word of caution is needed here, because once you show you have abandoned the ball you *must* proceed under the stroke-and-distance rule. Suppose you plunge into the undergrowth and snarl 'This is hopeless' and fight your way back to the fairway. And suppose that now your opponent, who we may assume has sportingly gone into the jungle with you calls out: 'Hello – here's a ball. What were you playing, a Dunlop 4? Oh what bad luck that you had already abandoned it. Really it's not lying too badly at all.'

Well, had you abandoned it? The rules of golf do not provide any official form of words for declaring a ball lost and your shout of 'This is hopeless' is ambiguous, to say the least. You will obviously want to play your ball while your opponent will insist that you had abandoned it as lost. The answer to this type of quandary – and we have another important example coming later in the matter of conceding putts – is to get into the habit of using a precise statement, rather like a Muslim husband discarding a wife with the declaration: 'I divorce thee, I divorce thee, I divorce thee.' There can be no doubt about your intentions if you say something along the lines of 'I hereby declare the (expletive deleted) ball lost and renounce all claim to it.' If we all made a habit of such positive statements, we could put an end to all the misunderstandings and bad blood which can flow from loose talk like: 'Oh bother! I suppose I'll have to go back and play another.'

A revealing example of the dangers inherent in this situation was provided in the British Open Championship of 1974 at Royal Lytham. The South African Dale Hayes hit into the wild, scrubby rough which is such a feature of linksland courses and after a short while (well inside his five minutes' grace) he left his fellow competitors to continue the search while he went back to the place from which he had played the shot. In effect, he was saving time and showing due consideration for golfers following behind, because he would now be ready to continue under the stroke-and-distance rule the moment his five minutes expired. He dropped another ball but before he played it – and still within his five minutes – a shout from the search area told him his original ball had been found. With a great feeling of relief he picked up the second ball and returned to play his original. He was later penalised because the moment he dropped another ball he legally abandoned his 'lost' ball and the second ball became the one in play. So the dropping of a ball is the vital act of abandonment, not the addressing or striking of it.

A number of misconceptions have grown up about how a player can abandon his ball. Many people believe that once you turn your back on the search area you have abandoned your ball. That is rubbish. You abandon your ball in three ways only – either by an unequivocal declaration (whether you search for it or not), or by the act of putting another ball into play, or by continuing play with your provisional ball beyond the point where your original ball is likely to be lost.

BALL MOVED (27)
Another danger of the hunt is that while you are thrashing about in the vegetation, you may very well accidentally move your ball. It is no use complaining that you didn't mean it and that where there is no guilty intention there can be no crime. The high principles of Roman law have no precedence in the rules of golf, and accidentally moving the ball, either directly

or causing it to move by touching anything (such as a fallen branch), comes into the category of our ghost strokes. You must add a penalty stroke to your score. But do not replace the ball in its original position. Remember the thinking behind the rule: you caused the ball to move and by adding a penalty stroke the effect is the same as if you had moved the ball with a deliberate stroke.

The same procedure applies if your partner or either of your caddies moves your ball accidentally during a search: take your penalty and play the ball from its new position. The reason for that little addition is obvious enough. An unscrupulous partner might 'accidentally' move your ball on purpose to give you a better lie and many caddies regard such a happy incident as no less than their duty.

However, if an opponent, or a fellow competitor in stroke play, or their caddies, or anyone not involved in the game, accidentally moves your ball there is no penalty and the ball must be replaced by you. The ghost stroke principle again provides the best way to remember this distinction. Clearly the accidental movement of your ball by a fellow competitor during a search cannot conceivably be construed as a stroke on your part. Therefore the ball must go back where it was. It should be carefully noted that we are talking about accidentally moving a ball *during a search*.

If a ball is accidentally moved in general play, a different set of rules apply but the principles remain the same.

Now, if your ball is accidentally moved by a match-play opponent, his caddie or equipment, then the opponent is considered to have played a ghost stroke at your ball and he is penalised a stroke. But since there could be times when it would be worth a penalty stroke 'accidentally' to kick your opponent's ball over a ravine, the ball must always be replaced by its owner. How strictly should this rule about accidentally moving a ball during a search be observed? If you are hunting in deep rough and inadvertently move your ball half an inch, or dislodge if from a precarious perch on a tuffet, does it really demand a penalty stroke? That is a question for each golfer to answer for himself, just one of the many occasions in golf when the player must be guided by his own conscience. However, there is one common mishap which often occurs during a search and which clearly causes the ball to move within the strict meaning of the rule. That is when you find the ball by stepping on it. You feel that welcome bulge under your foot and

I have found my ball all right but I accidentally kicked it. (What a pity it was not an opponent or fellow competitor who moved it during the search. Then you could have replaced it without penalty. As you accidentally moved it yourself it counts as one penalty stroke.)

shout 'Here's a ball.' Now while the ball nearly always moves by becoming further embedded into the turf, this is one occasion when most people agree that no penalty is warranted. Mind you, the rules of golf do not sanction this custom. The rules mean what they say. But in stepping on a ball, while it is obviously depressed, there is no way of determining that it did not revert to its original position when the weight of your foot was removed. So let us agree to an unofficial compact to penalise ourselves if we kick the ball but not simply if we step on it.

IDENTIFYING BALL (23)

Before we play on we must make sure that it really is our ball. Provided the ball is not in a hazard, this is one of the rare occasions when it is permissible to lift and place the ball. However, it can only be done for the purposes of identifying it (no cleaning, of course) and it must be done in the presence of your opponent or fellow competitor. The reason for the independent witness is to guarantee the next proviso: that the ball is replaced in its exact original position. If it is buried up to its waist in mud it must go back like that with no hanky panky about surreptitiously improving the lie under the guise of identifying it.

WRONG BALL (21)

It is important to identify your ball beyond doubt because there are harsh penalties to be paid for playing a wrong ball. These in themselves are an excellent reason for getting into the habit of carefully inspecting your ball before every shot – even when there is no possibility of doubt that it is yours. Obviously you do not lift to make this routine identification; you would become a highly suspicious character if you did that kind of thing, even though you were acting within the laws. But the habit of scrutinising your ball carefully on every shot saves you from the risk of playing a wrong ball and also helps your golf in that you absorb the details of its lie more thoroughly, and therefore produce the appropriate shot.

In match-play, if by chance you should happen to play a wrong ball (except in a hazard) you lose the hole. Your only hope of reprieve is if your opponent has also played a wrong ball and you can mutually determine that he played a wrong ball first. In that case he has lost the hole. And in those cases where players accidentally exchange balls during the play of a hole and they cannot discover who played a wrong ball first, then the hole must be played out with the exchanged balls.

In stroke play, if you play a wrong ball (again, except in a hazard) you add a two stroke penalty and then play your correct ball. Strokes played with the wrong ball do not count and if it happens to belong to a fellow competitor, it must be replaced. Of course, you may not notice that you have been playing a wrong ball until you hole out. Well, provided you have not hit off on the next tee, you can still follow the wrong-ball procedure, provided you can be sure of where you started to play the wrong ball. If you do not discover the error until you are playing the next hole (or have left the 18th green in the case of the last hole) then you must disqualify yourself because you have not completed the stipulated round in accordance with the rules.

BUNKERS AND WATER HAZARDS (33)

If you are in a hazard then you cannot lift your ball to identify it. All you can do if your ball is buried in loose sand, or under leaves, or such like, is to brush aside enough sand or other debris to determine that there is a golf ball of some kind down there. As soon as you detect a speck of white synthetic rubber, you have to stop. You have no divine right to a clear sight of your ball at any time in golf; you are only entitled to know the site of it. That applies everywhere but in a hazard it does not matter because in this one instance there is no penalty for playing a wrong ball. If you splash out of a bunker and discover that it wasn't your ball you played, you can go right back into the hazard and go on hitting any balls that you see until such time as you hit your own (21). That just about wraps up the lost-ball situation. If it can't be found after a five-minute search, or if you decide to abandon it as lost anyway, you either go back and play another under the stroke-and-distance rule or you continue play with your provisional ball if you have had the foresight to put one into play.

The one exception to these lost-ball procedures is if you hit one into a water hazard. There are two types of water hazard – ordinary and lateral – and they should be clearly defined in the local rules on the card of the course. So if you see your ball go into the water, the first thing to do is consult the card and discover if you are in ordinary water or lateral water. Mind you, your ball need not necessarily be immersed in water. Perhaps it is embedded in a bank or has disappeared down a deep fissure in the cracked mud of a pond which has not seen a drop of water for months. That makes no difference. If the local rule says it is water then water it is, wet or dry, and if your ball is within the defined boundaries of the hazard, you are in water. Of course, you may play the ball as it lies but, being in a hazard, you must not ground your club or remove any loose impediments. But let us assume that your ball is hopelessly immersed in water.

With an ordinary hazard you can proceed under the stroke-and-distance rule or you can take advantage of the one genuinely humane piece of legislation in the rule book. Not that compassion was the guiding motive behind the legislation. Never mind. Let us not question the motives too deeply just now. What you do is drop a ball, under penalty of one stroke, keeping the spot where the shot crossed its boundary between you and the hole. You can go as far back along that line as you like. In practice, of course, the most usual case is to drop as near to the water as possible so as to give yourself the shortest shot on your second attempt to carry the water.

Now we have the lateral water hazards which are usually ponds and ditches running roughly in the same direction as the line of play. Here you have the same two options as for a ball lost in an ordinary water hazard and another possibility as well. You can drop under penalty of one stroke within two club-lengths of *either* side of the hazard opposite the point where the shot crossed its boundary.

Finally, the ball may be lost in a hazard – and now we are talking about regular bunkers, not water hazards – in which there is an accumulation of casual water, snow, ground under repair, or scrapes caused by a burrowing animal. In that case you can drop another ball in the hazard *without penalty* (32) in an area which avoids interference from these special conditions either to your ball or your stance. Alternatively you can drop behind the hazard under penalty of one stroke.

4 INTERFERENCE

OUTSIDE AGENCIES: Ball at rest moved – Moving ball stopped or deflected – Stationary ball – INSIDE AGENCIES: Dropping the ball – Burrowing animals – Ground under repair – Casual water – On the green – Impediments and obstructions

Outside agencies

Golf courses are agreeable places, often quiet havens of greenery in industrial areas. They attract casual visitors who are there for purposes other than golf – to picnic, to stroll about enjoying the scenery, in the case of small boys to search for golf balls, and sometimes, notably when the course is part of a public park, for reasons which need not be too closely discussed here. By the same token, golf courses often teem with all manner of wild life. Indeed, one of the beneficial effects of golf is that courses serve as nature reserves where threatened species of bird, insect and animal life can flourish free of the growing dangers from poisonous agricultural pesticides.

For the golfer, however, these various forms of extraneous humanity and natural life are classified under the general heading of 'outside agency' (def 22). It is a dull and unimaginative expression to describe the full spectrum of mankind and wildlife, but there it is. If a rare golden eagle swoops down and snatches your ball in mid-flight, you, as a golfer, must suppress your ornithological excitement as best you may and think in terms of an outside agency. The author once watched in dismay while playing in the Danish Open Championship in Copenhagen as his ball was eaten by an outside agency in the form of a large red deer. Outside agencies can also be inanimate. A fellow competitor's golf ball can be an outside agency, as can a stray football kicked on to the course, and as too are spectators, referees, markers, fellow competitors and their caddies. The official definition describes an outside agency as *any agency not part of the match or, in stroke-play, not part of the competitor's side.*

The reason we must be quite sure of our grounds in recognising outside agencies is that they frequently affect our golf and it is important that the player should know what to do if his ball is carried off by a playful dog, or lands in a greenkeeper's pocket, or collides with another competitor's ball in mid-air.

BALL AT REST MOVED
The general rule through the green is that if your ball is stationary when it is moved by an outside agency you replace it. There is no penalty, of course, because the movement of the ball was none of your doing.

MOVING BALL STOPPED OR DEFLECTED
If your ball is moving when it is deflected or stopped by an outside agency, then you play it from where it comes to rest. Sometimes that is not possible. If your moving ball lodges in a moving outside agency, such as the talons of that golden eagle or the jaws of a dog, then obviously you cannot play it as it lies. In that event you drop a ball, without penalty, as near as you can judge to be the place where the outside agency took your ball. The procedure is different on the green. If a ball played on the green is in motion when it is stopped or deflected by an outside agency then that stroke is cancelled and the ball is replaced.

STATIONARY BALL
Confusion over the difference between the procedures for outside agencies influencing stationary and moving balls cost the South African Bobby Cole dearly in the British Open Championship at Hoylake in 1967. His ball had come to rest in a good lie near the green and a spectator running to get a good vantage point to watch the next shot kicked it into thick rough. Cole was not sure what to do about it so he relied on his instincts for sportsmanship and the spirit of the game. He had been brought up in the tradition that the ball must be played as it lies and so he felt that the safest thing to do was to play it from the long grass. It was a horribly difficult shot and cost him his par. Then, to make matters worse, he was penalised two strokes for not replacing his ball. Instead of a likely 4, or possible birdie 3, he ended up with a 7 for that hole.

As in the Tony Jacklin incident with the rabbit hole discussed in the introduction, Cole paid a high price for relying on his sense of sportsmanship. Incidentally, if an outside agency such as the spectator in the Bobby Cole incident moves your stationary ball, he is the best witness as to where it should be replaced. By all means let him point out the spot, but do not let him do the replacing. The rule requires the player to replace his ball and, as we have seen, in the rules of golf *every* word means what is says.

So much for the general rules governing outside agencies. Now let us consider some of the cases when your ball is moved or deflected by what we may describe as inside agencies, even if the rules of golf disdain to use such an expression.

Inside agencies

For our purposes here, inside agencies are people or equipment who are directly involved in our game of golf, either as partners, opponents, caddies and equipment. Note that a fellow competitor in a stroke-play event is not an inside agency. He is really nothing to do with you and counts as an outside agency if your ball is deflected by him or if he accidentally moves your ball. There is one important exception to that rule on the green and we will come to that later. For the moment we are concerned with play from tee to green and everything in this section will be concerned with play through the green. Some of the points have already been discussed in earlier sections, but no matter; a little repetition may help to make the lessons stick.

Stroke-play
First, let us look at inside agencies in stroke-play because the rules are simple (26). If your moving ball hits yourself (in a rebound for example) or your partner or either of your caddies or equipment, you suffer a penalty of two strokes. That's fair enough. After all, you have every control over your part of the game and it is clearly your fault if you hit anything. There is also a darker intention behind this rule. An unscrupulous caddie or partner could 'accidentally' deflect your shot to your advantage. Hence the dire penalty of two strokes. In the same way, if an outside agency or fellow competitor should 'accidentally' move your stationary ball there is no penalty. You replace your ball and play on.

SAME INCIDENT, DIFFERENT PENALTIES
Match-play: What bad luck! You lose the hole, I am afraid.
Stroke-play: Pity you didn't duck in time – you must add a penalty shot to your score.

Now for a brief résumé of the procedures to follow if your stationary ball is moved, in both match- and stroke-play.

By an outside agency. Replace it with no penalty.

During a search by an opponent, fellow competitor or their caddies: replace it. No penalty.

Accidentally by yourself, partner or your caddies, or by touching anything which causes the ball to move: one penalty stroke and play it as it lies from its new position.

After you have addressed the ball except on tee: one penalty stroke and play it as it lies.

In touching a loose impediment within a club-length of your ball: one penalty stroke and play it where it lies.

Match-play

In match-play the rules are slightly different and the best way to remember the distinction is to bear in mind the possibilities which could be provoked by the murkier depths of human nature in the heat of battle. So if your moving ball is deflected or stopped by your opponent (or his caddie or equipment) then the opponent loses the hole (26). That should be sufficient to stop him 'accidentally' getting in the way of one of your brilliant shots. But if we ascribe such dubious motives to the enemy, then we must assume ourselves to be capable of stooping just as low – like, for example, getting out of a difficult situation by placing our clubs in such a position as to stop the ball rolling into a bunker. Therefore, if your ball hits anything to do with you – yourself, your partner, your caddie or your equipment, then you lose the hole.

The fiendish plot might occur to you deliberately to knock your ball against an opponent's bag and claim the hole. The laws do not specifically forbid such uncouth behaviour, which is one very good reason for keeping yourself and your equipment well clear of the line of fire. But a committee might well punish such unsportsmanlike conduct under Rule 1.

We have already gone over the possibilities and procedures when you move your stationary ball. If your opponent (caddie and equipment) accidentally moves your stationary ball, he suffers a penalty stroke and you replace your ball.

The only exception to all this is the rare instance when your ball hits and

SAME INCIDENT, DIFFERENT PENALTIES

Match-play: Oh! A shank! Still, it does win the hole for me.

Stroke-play: It may be a rub of the ankle for you but it is a rub of the green for me. I suffer no penalty for hitting a fellow competitor and must play the ball as it lies.

moves your opponent's ball (remember, we are not yet on the green). In that case, there is no penalty, which neatly disposes of the dastardly possibility that when your balls lay close together you could knock yours against his and claim the hole. Bad luck, they've thought of that one. So there is no penalty and, what's more, your opponent has the option of replacing his ball or playing it as it lies in its new position.

Outside agencies often intervene on big occasions when the course is swarming with spectators. Some golfers deliberately overhit their approaches to the greens which are screened at the back by solid walls of human flesh, confident of a rebound from shin or foot. At the US Masters at Augusta, a large bank behind the 18th green makes a natural grandstand and it is a favourite place for spectators to sit and watch the play. One year an approach shot rolled up the skirt of a woman who was sitting by the green. She jumped up and disappeared into the crowd with the ball still lodged on her person. Since the golfer was patently unable to play the ball from where it came to rest, an official awarded a free drop.

One outside agency which played a vital part in a competition was a lamb. During a club tournament at Burton-on-Trent in 1928 a competitor's ball was rolling up the edge of the green when the lamb picked it up in its mouth and neatly deposited it into the hole. But what are we to make of the case in which at the moment a player's ball dropped into the hole a large frog jumped out, knocking the ball out with it? The answer to that one is a question of fact according to Definition 4: *A ball is 'holed' when it lies within the circumference of the hole and all of it is below the level of the lip of the hole.*

DROPPING THE BALL
We have already touched on some of the occasions when a golfer may have to put a ball into play by dropping it. Dropping is a common experience for golfers and before going on to consider other occasions when dropping may be needed, we might pause briefly over the actual procedure of dropping. (Remember the general rule that when putting a ball into play you may tee it up if you are on the teeing ground; you drop it through the green or in a hazard; and you place it on the green.)

The procedure for dropping a ball sounds deceptively simple. You stand up straight facing the hole and drop the ball over your shoulder. However, there are pitfalls even in this straightforward situation. Let us imagine an

Should the ball drop cleanly to the ground and then rebound against any part of you, then the ball is in play. You do not re-drop.

unscrupulous player who sees an inviting patch of turf just outside the limit of his dropping area. He might conceive a plan to drop the ball and deflect it in mid-flight with a well-timed shimmy of his posterior. The lawmakers have thought of that one. If the ball touches any part of the golfer or his clothing on its descent it must be re-dropped without penalty. That proviso, incidentally, solves the dilemma of the winter golfer who was wearing an anorak and dropped his ball into the hood . . . Once the ball has hit the ground, however, it must not be re-dropped if it should bounce against the player's foot. Once it is on the ground, with the exceptions that we shall look at in a moment, it is in play.

The nature of the occasions on which a player has to drop his ball often means that it is rough undulating territory and the ball frequently rolls away. It is here that for once the golfer's instinct for fair play can betray him. Usually in golf a player will not go far wrong if he abides by the common-sense solution to his dilemma but in dropping a ball it may roll a few feet into a much more favourable position. The golfer who tells himself that he is now taking an unfair advantage from a lucky bounce and re-drops his ball is in trouble. Unless the ball has rolled nearer the hole, it is in play *within two club-lengths of the point where it landed* and the moment the player touches that ball he is liable to a two stroke penalty (or loss of hole).

The fair-play convention applies in all other cases. For example, if you are dropping a ball in a hazard and it rolls out, you re-drop in the hazard. Hard luck. But you may be dropping and see your ball roll into a hazard. Apply the common-sense solution and re-drop without penalty outside the hazard. The same applies to a ball rolling out of bounds. Re-drop. Sometimes the ground is so uneven that the ball would not come to rest within the permitted area if you went on dropping it all day. In that case, after trying two drops, you can place the ball in the correct position.

To summarise, there are four situations in which you can re-drop without penalty: if the ball touches you during its descent; if it rolls nearer the hole; if it rolls more than two club-lengths from its point of impact; if it rolls out of bounds or into a hazard (or out of a hazard if this is where you are trying to drop it).

The situation to impress firmly on the mind is that one about two club-lengths because many golfers are confused as to their rights. Say you are entitled to a free drop from a rabbit hole. You drop two club-lengths clear of

If you suffer from (or even enjoy) the condition known as lordosis, involving an excessively hollowed back and prominent backside, your ball may strike your person as it drops. In that case you must re-drop.

the rabbit hole and your ball can roll a further two club-lengths away, making a possible relief of four club-lengths in all.

A further complication can arise in dropping. Say a player has taken a drop from an unplayable lie and on dropping his ball it rolls less than two club-lengths but into ground under repair or behind an immovable obstruction. Well, the answer is simply to follow the logic of the situation. The drop was correctly performed and the ball is in play so now the golfer can take relief with another drop, possibly in quite a different place, under the rules governing ground under repair or obstructions. However, with the best will in the world it sometimes happens that a player drops, or places, his ball under an appropriate rule and then, after he has played his next shot, discovers that the drop, or placing, was made in the wrong place. That mishap carries the standard penalty of two strokes or loss of hole.

BURROWING ANIMALS

The golfer is a lonely creature. He is not a member of a team with comrades to encourage and help him. He is all by himself with nothing but his own resources to fight the good fight against the tyrant golf ball. But if the golfer can look to no man for help (except from his caddie, if he has one, and even then the assistance must be limited to advice and encouragement), he may often find an ally among the dumb creatures of the field. So never scorn the snake in the grass, or the rabbit, or the delicate sand piper which builds its nest by tunnelling into the ground. If your ball should come to rest in a hole or scrape or pile of earth made by such burrowing animals, or indeed if your stance or swing is affected by such natural inconveniences, then you can drop your ball clear within two club-lengths (not nearer the hole, of course) without penalty (32). Once again a word of caution must be sounded. The rules here are, as always, to be taken literally. Birds, reptiles and burrowing animals mean exactly that and no more, and does not include the whole range of fauna. And that is bad luck on golfers who play in tropical climates where ants abound and may build vast cathedrals 10 ft. high. The rules of golf do not extend to the insect world and ant hills offer the golfer no opportunity for relief. The only course is to fall back on the unplayable-ball rule (29) and spend a penalty stroke or to take courage in both hands, play the ball as it lies, and risk a multiple injection of formic acid from an army of maddened ants. In some places the ant hill also commonly does double duty as the home of the king cobra and an injudicious blow with your wedge could provoke a situation which might test the loyalty of your friends to the limit.

GROUND UNDER REPAIR (def 13)

Exactly the same rules cover ground under repair and casual water. Ground under repair, commonly marked with notices simply stating 'GUR', may be any part of the course which the committee feels to be unfit for golf, such as a newly seeded area, or ground mashed up by tractor ruts, or even patches of rough land. In that case the GUR will be clearly marked or defined in the local rules on the card. Some courses, for example, rule that gravel paths provided for golf carts are GUR. In addition, and without any special marking, material piled for removal and holes made by greenkeepers are automatically GUR. That expression 'material piled for removal' is widely cited by unscrupulous golfers seeking a free drop and there was once a scoundrel of a caddie who carried a small bag of grass clippings with him. Whenever his man had a bad lie, this caddie would surreptitiously sprinkle a handful of clippings onto the ball, and then urge his player to avail himself of the GUR loop-hole.

An element of common sense is needed in deciding whether you are entitled to free drop. The words 'piled for removal' clearly imply that there must be a definite pile. If the greenkeeper has strewn the cuttings over a wide area then obviously he has no intention of removing them. Also, if the cuttings are old, brown and rotting, then it is fair to assume that whatever the intention may have been in the first case, the material is no longer destined for removal.

CASUAL WATER (def 8)

As for the casual water, the definition says that it must be visible before or after you have taken your stance. In practice if you stand by your ball and water oozes up by the welt of your golf shoe, then you can claim relief. The water must be temporary, of course, but it would include an overflow from a regular water hazard provided it was outside the defined boundary of the hazard.

Snow and ice are included in the definition but they may also be treated as loose impediments, entirely at the discretion of the golfer. One excessively devious golfer sought relief from such conditions by saying that while he was a right-hander, he wanted to play that particular shot left-handed – and in that case his stance was affected by a puddle. He wanted a free drop and the incident was put to the Rules of Golf Committee for judgement.

It was decided that the golfer was entitled to his drop, there being no restriction on ambidexterity, provided that he then actually played a left-handed shot.

By now there should be no confusion about the slight variations in procedure in hazards on the green. If you are in casual water, GUR or burrowing animal scrape in a bunker, you drop in the bunker – or if you prefer you can drop outside the bunker for a penalty shot. If your ball is lost in such conditions in a bunker, then you drop another ball in the bunker without penalty.

ON THE GREEN

On the green there is an extra element of relief. Here your ball or stance do not have to be directly affected. Provided the casual water, animal scrape or GUR interferes with the line of your putt, you may place your ball on the nearest spot which gives you maximum relief, although you must never place your ball nearer the hole. The idea is to remove the source of sheer bad luck which has befallen you by a chance of nature, not to give positive help.

IMPEDIMENTS AND OBSTRUCTIONS

An area of confusion for many people is the distinction between loose impediments and obstructions, which is which, and what can you do about them. The simple rule of thumb is that impediments are objects made by nature; obstructions are objects made by man. So impediments include fallen twigs, leaves, loose stones, worm casts and rabbit dung. 'Loose' means that the object is not fixed, not growing and not adhered to the ball. Obstructions would cover such debris as discarded drink cans and cigarette packets (both of which ought to be deposited in litter baskets but are all too often just thrown down at random these days). A thoughtlessly discarded bottle once tragically may have cost the Irishman Harry Bradshaw an Open Championship, which should serve as a potent reminder to us all to curb any litter-bug tendencies. Other common examples of obstructions would be greenkeeper's equipment, or fence posts protecting plantations of young trees and hedges. So if the club captain had an air shot and collapsed with mortification on the 4th fairway, his inert body would be a loose impediment but the club which had fallen from his hand would be an obstruction. Roads and paths, with their curbs, and anything used to define the boundary of the course are not obstructions. Most courses contain buildings used for course-maintenance equipment, or telegraph poles or some such extraneous objects. The committee has the power to decide which, if any, of these things are to be defined as integral parts of the course. In that case the fact will be clearly stated on the card of the course and they are not obstructions. Sprinkler heads, now standard equipment on most courses, are normally classified as obstructions and if one interferes with the lie of your ball or your stance, you can drop two club-lengths clear without penalty.

Loose impediments (48)
The simpler of these two problems is the loose impediment. In essence, you are allowed to move any debris which qualifies as a loose impediment, with no penalty, except when both the ball and the impediment are in a hazard. So a big stone can be thrown out of the way, a broken branch can be hauled clear and fallen leaves and fir cones can be cleared. By the same token, if you have occasion to lift your ball, say under the unplayable-ball rule or from ground under repair, and the area on to which you are required to drop is covered by a loose impediment, you can move it before you make your drop. Of course, you could similarly move the impediments *after* dropping but that would not be the best procedure because of the danger that in moving the impediment you might accidentally move the ball. That is one of our ghost shots and you would be liable to a penalty stroke.

The other important point to bear in mind is that the impediment must be loose. If, for example, your ball lay on hard-packed sand you would be entirely out of order to pick away with your finger-nail at the sand behind the ball. That would constitute illegally improving the lie. Sand and loose soil are only impediments on the green.

Obstructions (31)
The general rule with obstructions is that if you can move the obstruction you do so and if it is too heavy or firmly fixed into the ground you move the ball, even in hazards or on the green. No matter. Obstructions are really artifacts which are superfluous to the game of golf and therefore you are entitled

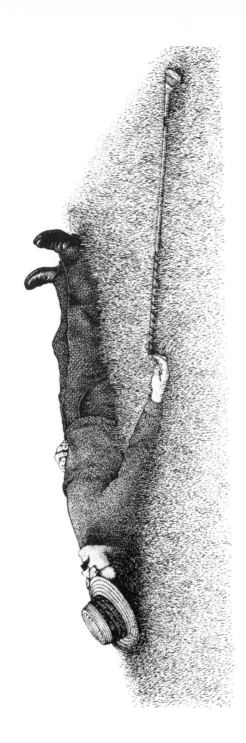

Distinguish between loose impediments and movable obstructions. The hat and the club which has fallen from the inert grasp of a collapsed golfer are man-made, therefore obstructions. The member himself is a loose impediment. If you had the misfortune to come upon this scene in a bunker you could remove the hat and club but would have to leave the member. After playing out of the sand, and provided you did not unduly hold up play, you might try the kiss of life on him. It sometimes works.

to relief from them without penalty. If your ball happens to move while you are lifting an obstruction, there is no penalty (unlike in the case when moving an impediment) and you replace the ball in its original lie.

One of the hoary old stories of golf which has been handed down from generation to generation is that the way to beat a Scotsman is to wait until his ball lands in a bunker. Then you craftily throw a coin into the bunker and the Scot, by definition a thrifty creature, will not be able to stop himself from falling on the coin with cries of delight at his good fortune. Even as he slips it into his pocket you inform him that he has incurred a two stroke penalty. It is not a very funny story and has absolutely no validity in golf law since a coin, being man-made, is an obstruction and it can be removed from the hazard with impunity. So don't waste your money on that dodge.

But while obstructions normally give the golfer no cause for worry, there is one facet of the rule which does create friction. Golfers get it into their heads that they are entitled to relief from obstructions and they seem to imagine that this means complete freedom to drop in a position which gives them a completely clear shot. And there they make a big mistake. Many a card has been ruined by disqualification because of an excessively liberal view of the obstruction concession. So let us look at what the rule says with some care. If the obstruction is movable, as for instance the grass box of a lawn-mower, you can move it regardless of where your ball may be. A hose-pipe used for water on greens is another common example. If it is in the line of the shot, move it – although in that particular example it is only proper that you put it back the way it was after you have completed the hole. But if it is immovable – say a greenkeeper's shed or an electricity pylon – and your ball lies so close to it that the obstruction interferes with your stance or restricts your intended swing, then you are entitled to a free drop. You must determine the nearest point which allows a clear swing and then measure off two club-lengths from that spot. So if you are behind a shed, it may still loom in front of you after you have dropped your two club-lengths. This is just your bad luck. The rule is not intended to give you a clear shot, only to give you room to make a full swing. You have no right to a clear line of vision for your shot. You will still have to play round the shed or try a do-or-die effort to loft your ball over it.

The only exception to this harsh judgement is if you happen to find your ball against an obstruction so that it is behind you, interfering with your backswing. Now there is nowhere for you to drop which is not nearer the hole, and we know by now that the ball must never be dropped or allowed to roll nearer the hole. In that case you can go to the nearest side of the obstruction and measure off two club-lengths from there.

One of the rare examples in the rules of golf which demonstrates a hint of humanity within the stony hearts of the lawmakers concerns bird-nests. By the definition we have been discussing, the nests of birds full of eggs or fledgelings must be loose impediments, since they are quite clearly natural objects not fixed or growing and not adhering to the ball. Yet the rules of golf say otherwise. There is no need for vandalism if your ball lands near a bird's nest. It has been specially classified as an immovable obstruction, entirely contrary to the letter and spirit of the definition, and you may drop two club-lengths clear without a moment's hesitation to consider whether you would be justified in making an omelette of a clutch of plover's eggs in order to save your par.

There was one famous case of the machinations of the obstruction rule when a player in a championship hit his ball through the club-house window. There was no local rule defining the club-house as out of bounds or an integral part of the course, so the player, with admirable aplomb, strode into the smoking room, asked for a window to be opened, and played the ball back to the green. The window, in his view, was a movable obstruction. The appeal judges gave weighty deliberation to this case and finally decided that by opening the window the player should have incurred a two stroke penalty for improving the line of his play. The window was a part of an immovable obstruction and should not have been moved. It would have been perfectly in order for the golfer to have moved a chair or table but not the window.

Oddly enough, in a parallel case with a loose impediment, the ruling went the other way. A large branch fell from a tree and it was decided to be quite proper for a player to break off a small branch. As for the question of what is movable, that is up to you and the power of your biceps. In one competition a player's ball landed against a heavy branch which had been brought down in a storm. Since he could not move this loose impediment he declared his ball unplayable and dropped clear under penalty. Another player had the same predicament later in the day. With the help of some husky caddies he managed to drag the branch clear and it was ruled that he had been perfectly in order to do so.

5 HAZARDS

BUNKERS: Grounding the club – Finding the ball – Obstructions and impediments – Casual water, ball lost or unplayable – Smoothing the sand – WATER HAZARDS: Lateral water hazards – Water-hazard rules – EXAMPLES

In the course of discussing the different rules of golf we have touched on most of the regulations governing hazards, if only by way of mentioning that exceptional procedures apply to hazards. So this chapter will necessarily cover much of the ground we have already covered. There is no harm in that. Repetition is one way of learning the rules and it will be helpful to retrace our steps through the bunkers of golf law and smooth out any irregularities of misconceptions and doubt.

The first thing to get absolutely clear is what the rules mean by a hazard. Golf-course architects in their infinite cunning present the golfer with all manner of obstacles. The inviting swathe of mown fairway is interrupted or bounded by features of special difficulty for the golfer to negotiate and they are not all hazards by any means. The rules define the two varieties of hazard: bunkers and water hazards. Let us start with the bunker.

Bunkers

Golfers commonly use the words 'hazard' and 'bunker' (and 'trap') as different ways of saying the same thing. The rules are more precise. Bare patches, scrapes, roads, tracks and paths are not hazards – and they are not ground under repair either, unless specifically marked. The official definition of a bunker calls it *an area of bare ground, often a depression, which is usually covered with sand.* Recalling that important provision that every word in the rules means what it says, we can now look at the definition and see that the grass-covered banks of bunkers are not part of the bunker. The rules go on to make that very point and further make it clear that islands of grass within a bunker, such as the famous tuffets at Pebble Beach are not part of the hazard.

The vital factor is the presence of grass. Grass surroundings, or islands of grass, or grass banks are not part of the bunker. Nor are artificial bankings, usually made of stone or wood, which are found on some courses.

Many courses have grassy depressions, in some cases legacies of wartime bomb craters which the clubs have left to grow over and remain. Sometimes they are provided by the architect as landscaping features. Others occur naturally. We golfers loosely refer to them as 'grass bunkers', an expression we now know to be a contradiction in terms. They are not hazards under the rules so if you play a wrong ball from such a 'grass bunker' you are not entitled to immunity from penalty. You must follow the standard wrong-ball procedure.

GROUNDING THE CLUB (33)

Having got that point clear, we can immediately settle one of the oldest arguments in golf. This subject produces long, noisy altercations in club bars every week, namely: What happens if a golfer touches anything with his club during the backswing of his stroke in a bunker? The rules say that before making a stroke the player shall not touch the ground in a hazard with a club or otherwise. So what happens if you brush the sand with your clubhead on the backswing? And is it the same if you touch the grass on the banking? The answer is that touching the grass (or stone or wood banking) involves no infringement since it is not part of the hazard. Touching the sand on your backswing is an offence since 'a stroke' is defined as a forward motion of the club and you have thus touched the ground before making a stroke. The general penalty applies – two shots penalty or loss of hole in match play. Let further argument cease.

For this reason it is a sound plan to play sand shots with a steep uplift of the club in order to avoid the risk of brushing the sand on the backswing. Fortunately, most teachers prescribe this method as the best technique for sand shots anyway.

FINDING THE BALL

Let us recap the rules about finding your ball in a hazard. You can brush aside enough sand or leaves or other debris to determine the presence of a

But grass bordering a bunker, or even growing within the bunker, is not part of the hazard and if your club brushes it on the backswing then there is no penalty. In the same way, wooden bunker facings, or walls, are not part of the hazard and there is no penalty for touching them on the backswing.

golf ball. It need not necessarily be yours and you are not entitled to uncover it sufficiently to identify it as such. Do not fret; there is no penalty for playing a wrong ball provided you then go back and play the right one, and such shots with a wrong ball do not count either.

OBSTRUCTIONS AND IMPEDIMENTS

Having found your ball, or a ball, you are at liberty to remove any obstructions (artificial objects such as cigarette packets and soft-drink cans). What you must not do is touch any loose impediments (natural objects like leaves and twigs) except by the minimum amount necessary to discover a buried ball. And you must not touch the surface of the sand with your club or hand to test the surface or in any way improve the lie of the ball. Your only entitlement is to ground your feet firmly in taking your stance. That should be enough to give you all the information you need about the consistency of the lie for you to plan the type of shot to play.

You may be wondering why you can move loose impediments through the green but not when they are in, or touching, a hazard. It sounds a bit of an anomaly. Not really. The spirit of golf (which the rules seek to protect) is that hazards should be exactly that – nasty places to be avoided if possible and difficult to escape from without dropping a shot. Many professionals forget that concept. They play sand shots so well that they expect to play out of bunkers without detriment to their scores. They complain bitterly about a bad lie in a bunker having cost them a stroke. You are expected to get a bad lie in a hazard – that's why they are filled with soft sand or water. You are supposed to avoid hazards; they are deliberately sited to punish a bad shot. No sympathy is called for in the case of a bad lie in a hazard and complaints about the rough conditions in hazards should be ignored. Oakmont, the famous American championship course, has a machine specially designed to plough furrows in bunkers and guarantee a positively bad lie every time.

Similar strictures apply to the design of pot bunkers just big enough and deep enough, in the immortal phrase of the late Bernard Darwin, 'to hold an angry man and his mashie'. If you get into one of these fairway pot bunkers at St Andrews, you might as well abandon all hope of getting onto the green; often enough you will be doing well to get back onto the fairway with your recovery stroke.

CASUAL WATER, BALL LOST OR UNPLAYABLE

We can now look briefly once more at the other rules governing hazards. In a bunker, if your ball lies in casual water, ground under repair or casts made by burrowing animals, or if these conditions interfere with your stance or the area of your intended swing, you may take relief in the normal way by dropping a ball, without penalty, in the bunker on a spot which gives maximum relief from these conditions. Or you can drop a ball outside the bunker for one penalty stroke. If your ball is lost in such conditions in a hazard – and you must have good reasons for believing it to be lost – you may drop another ball in the hazard in the same manner, again without penalty. You can declare your ball unplayable in a bunker but in that case you may not invoke the full range of unplayable-ball options. You can only drop a ball in the bunker under penalty of one stroke. If you lose a ball in a bunker you have to adopt the stroke-and-distance procedure.

SMOOTHING THE SAND

Hazards impose special obligations on golfers under the etiquette of the game. The player whose ball goes into a bunker is often an angry man, and when we lose our tempers we often lose our good manners as well. It is no less than common courtesy to smooth out your footprints after playing out of bunkers and on that subject a short digression is in order, in the form of a plea to tournament players.

All of us are conditioned in our golfing behaviour to some degree by what we see on television or in the person of the great players. We copy their mannerisms – the bad ones as well all too often – at the same time as we try to copy their swings. The process may be subconscious but it is a fact and it puts a responsibility on the stars which they are not always quick to acknowledge or accept.

Slow play, the bane of golf, obviously derives to a large extent from this process of aping the great players, particularly their tedious dithering over putts. In the present context of bunker play, how often do you see a tournament professional play out of a bunker beside the green and then clamber up the face, using his wedge like a climbing pick and imprinting deep footmarks in the sand? He knows that there is an employee standing by – but probably out of shot – with a rake to restore the bunker to its pristine condition. But the TV viewer will retain that image of the mountaineering golfer leaving

If there is a rake provided by a bunker it is only sensible to take it with you as you go into the sand to play your shot. But do not stick it into the sand like this – that is testing the condition of the surface.

But you are perfectly entitled to take the rake with you and lay it down on the sand. In the same way, if you are carrying your own clubs it is permissible to lay the bag down in the sand while you play your shot.

the bunker looking like a battlefield and he may do the same thing in his own golf – when there is no rake man there to tidy up after him. How much more thoughtful it would be if the professionals made a point always of smoothing their footprints (if only by token gestures) and by retracing their steps in the prescribed manner out of the back of the bunker. Then we would all subconsciously get the message of the correct form.

The rules do not oblige you to smooth your footprints after playing your shot; they simply say that there is no penalty if you do so, provided you do nothing to improve the lie of your ball or help your subsequent play of the hole.

That rule had to be scrutinised with some care by officials at the 1969 US Masters when Arnold Palmer played a shot in a bunker, failed to get out and then angrily swung his club again, splashing it into the sand in a 'replay' of his original stroke. A referee penalised him two strokes for grounding his club in a bunker. Palmer was not happy with that ruling and sought advice from an official of the United States Golf Association. A committee meeting was hurriedly called and before the round was completed Palmer was told that the penalty had been rescinded. That decision caused a fine old controversy. Clearly the committee had been guided by the spirit of the rules which are designed to prevent the player from improving his lie or helping him in his play. But many people felt that the referee had been quite right in imposing the penalty, particularly in view of a decision (no 64/108/241) by the Rules of Golf Committee in a similar case. That decision reads, in part: 'Rule 33–1 is mandatory in that when a player is about to play out of a bunker he is not permitted to touch the ground in a hazard before making his stroke. After making a stroke in a hazard he must ensure that he is not required immediately to play another stroke from that hazard before he touches the ground with his club.' Palmer got the benefit of the considerable doubt in that case and the best advice is never to replay a stroke in a bunker, in hot or cold blood.

A rather different incident was put to the Rules of Golf Committee when a player accidentally dropped his club in the sand before playing. Here justice prevailed with the ruling that no penalty was due. Another famous incident was the action of Tom Weiskopf in the last round of a tournament which he happened to be leading. In that tense situation he wanted to be absolutely certain of his yardages for a critical approach shot. He therefore marched purposefully forward on a bee-line to the flag and his path took him straight through the middle of a greenside bunker. Having completed his yardage count, Weiskopf retraced his steps and on the way back he meticulously smoothed away his footprints in the bunker. The question now arose: had he improved his line for his subsequent play of the hole? It was ruled that he had not. At most he had restored the line to its original condition, although the officials might have found this decision more difficult if Weiskopf had then played into that bunker. They might have then felt justified in ruling that the surface had been tested before making the stroke. In the actual event, they had no great problem in exonerating Weiskopf, although some people felt at the time that a general penalty might have been warranted on the grounds of unduly delaying play.

Water hazards

A water hazard is officially any sea, lake, pond, river, ditch, surface drainage ditch or other open water course, regardless of whether or not it contains water. Any island of land is part of the hazard. Now while the banks of a bunker are not part of the hazard, the same is clearly not true of a water hazard. The water level of a pond may have fallen, or dried up completely, leaving a grassy bank and that most definitely *is* in the hazard. It is the duty of the committee to define clearly the limits of water hazards and this is usually done by means of coloured stakes or lines.

LATERAL WATER HAZARDS
A lateral water hazard fulfills all the above conditions. It lies more or less in the direction of the line of play, thus making it impossible to drop a ball behind it. Once again it is up to the committee to define the lateral water hazards in a clear and distinctive manner because a slightly different procedure has to be used with them.

WATER-HAZARD RULES
Now water hazards. If your ball goes into a hazard, you are at liberty to play it as it lies, of course. This is an option which many golfers never consider, although professionals often take off their shoes and socks and wade into the water to play wonderful recoveries. Lu Liang Huan, the Formosan who

came so close to winning the British Open at Royal Birkdale in 1971, played a masterly stroke from water several inches deep in the last round of the Moroccan Grand Prix of 1974. Unfortunately, as at Birkdale, he came second on that occasion, so we cannot describe his aquatic shot as a winner.

The Barcelona Golf Club, El Prat, has a water hazard which is designed to tempt the player to have a go. The water is kept at a depth of just over an inch, so it is a fair gamble for the golfer to chance his arm and risk soaking himself in the club-head's bow-wave.

Wet or dry, you must not ground your club in a water hazard. (If the ball is in muddy water you can rake about with a club to find it and there is no penalty if you move the ball, provided you either replace it or take lawful relief under penalty.)

Perhaps you do not care to risk it. Well, if your ball is in a water hazard – and it need not be in actual water, as we have seen – you may drop a ball either under stroke and distance or anywhere behind the hazard, on a line keeping the point where your ball crossed the margin of the hazard between you and the hole. You have to pay a one shot penalty, of course, and you adopt the identical procedure if your ball is lost in the water hazard.

Obviously you may not be able to drop a ball behind a lateral water hazard because, by definition, the direction of the lateral water hazard may make that impossible. So, provided that the hazard is clearly defined as a 'lateral', you may drop under penalty under the normal water-hazard rules or, in addition, within two club-lengths on either side of the hazard opposite the point at which your ball went in.

Examples

The best way to learn a rule is through the hard example of personal experience. It can take years to acquire your knowledge that way, and the purpose of this book is to short-circuit that painful process. So the next best thing is to provide some examples so that you can identify with the players and benefit from their experiences at second hand.

The examples which follow are all based on decisions which have been handed down on appeal by the Rules of Golf committees. Let us start with an incident which probably sounded hilarious to the player's friends when they heard about it, but which was clearly no joke to the player at the time. His ball lay in a water hazard, on a bank, and he decided to play it. Alas, he hit it out of bounds. Now, under the stroke-and-distance rule, he had to drop onto that bank. You can guess what happened – the ball rolled down the bank (less than two club-lengths) into the water.

The question – and how we can sympathise with the agonised player – was whether he had to take two spoonfuls of penalty medicine or whether, in the name of Christian charity and simple justice and the principles of double jeopardy, he might just this once be allowed to place his ball on the bank? In these multiple-disaster cases, it is important to keep a cool head and follow the horrendous sequence step by step, applying the appropriate rules as we go along. Having hit a ball out of bounds the player had no option but to follow the stroke-and-distance course. That is past history by the time he came to drop on the bank and cannot influence anything which might happen. The fact of having just gone out of bounds is irrelevant to the dropping situation. So when his ball rolled down into the water, he had no recourse but to bite on the bullet and pay another penalty to retrieve it under the water-hazard rules.

Two balls are in a bunker and while the first player is taking his shot, the other player stands in the bunker well away from his ball and leans on his club. Is he guilty of grounding his club? Yes, of course he is. That was too easy. Right. Take the same situation. Instead of leaning on his club, this time the second player takes a firm stance, still well away from his ball, and simulates the shot he is going to play but without using a club. Is he guilty of any offence? Indeed he is, said the committee. By taking what we might call a practice stance, he was unlawfully testing the condition of the surface.

In a foursome match, a player failed to get out of a bunker with his recovery shot. Now it was his partner's turn to play a bunker shot. But before leaving the bunker, the first player smoothed out his footprints. The opposition claimed the hole on the grounds that the partnership had grounded a club before playing the second bunker shot. Not at all, answered the adjudicators. Provided the lie of the ball was not improved, there was no penalty.

A player hit into a fast-moving stream. By the time he reached the hazard, the current had swept the ball downstream and out of bounds. What should he do? That's another fairly easy one. The rule is related specifically to *the spot at which the ball last crossed the margin of the water hazard*. It is immaterial that the ball was subsequently carried out of bounds.

Try this one. In a four-ball match a divot from one player's shot landed on top of his partner's ball, which lay in a bunker. The first player removed his divot and replaced it, as all golfers should do on (nearly) every occasion. Was the first player at fault in removing his divot (loose impediment) from the bunker? And was his partner guilty of any offence? Yes, they were both guilty, replied the committee with, one cannot help feeling, some relish. The first player was due a penalty for removing a loose impediment from the bunker. His partner was equally to blame under the rule that if a player breaks a rule which might help his partner's play, the partner incurs the relative penalty as well. Thus with an elegant left and right, the Rules of Golf Committee killed two birds with one divot. However, said the committee, having had its malicious fun, in stroke-play it would have ruled differently. Then the second player would have the right to move the divot off his ball under the principle that a player is normally entitled to the lie that his shot gave him, and to relief from the results of actions by fellow competitors and outside agencies. By the same token, an *opponent's* divot could have been removed in match-play.

A player 'thinned' his bunker shot and the ball shot over the green in that sickening way which every golfer knows all too well. He then replayed the shot twice, taking plenty of sand the way he should have done the first time. Now, however, it was discovered that his ball had gone out of bounds and he had to drop under stroke and distance in that bunker. Had he tested the surface with those practice swings? Yes, he had, ruled the committee. It was the player's responsibility to ensure that he was not going to have to play his next shot from the bunker before he took those practice swings.

A player whose ball lay in a hazard made two deliberate practice swings, taking a divot each time. 'That is only two penalty strokes,' he said. 'It does not matter how many practice strokes I took, I broke only one rule.' His marker thought that four penalty strokes were due. So, in the fullness of time, did the Rules of Golf Committee. If a player *inadvertently* breaks a rule more than once in the same incident, it is usual to let him off with the penalty for a single offence. For deliberately committing two separate offences, this player should be clobbered with the full sentence of four penalty strokes.

On that happy note, let us be done with hazards, smooth out our footprints and move on to the next phase of the game.

6 ON THE GREEN

Pitch marks – Impediments – Touching the line – Flagsticks – Croquet putting – Ball overhanging hole – Marking the ball – Concessions – Ball on the wrong green – Casual water

Putting is often called 'a game within a game' and the expression is doubly apt. It is true in the physical sense that after the *Donner und Blitzen* of golf through the green, straining every muscle to pour power into majestic drives and towering iron shots, the golfer must now change character and adopt the delicate approach of a watchmaker, bringing all his command of eye and touch and feeling into play with subtlety and fine precision. This contrast, more pronounced than in any other game, gives golf its unique distinction and charm as well, some might think, as its chief source of frustration. What changes we might have seen in the roll of the great champions if putting had not been of such paramount importance to the score.

Putting is also a game within a game in golf law. There are some significant departures from usual golfing principles as soon as your ball reaches the green and that, incidentally, means when any part of your ball touches the prepared putting surface.

PITCH MARKS (35)

You are now ready to putt and before you do so there are a number of things you can do to improve your chances of success. You can repair pitch marks made by the impact of balls landing on the green. As a matter of good golfing manners, you should always repair your own pitch mark and if you get a chance to repair such craters left by golfers less thoughtful than yourself, then by all means do so, provided you do not dally on the green and unduly hold up play.

Make absolutely certain that the damage you are repairing is a pitch mark. The bane of modern golf with watered greens and deep cleats on golf shoes is the proliferation of spike marks in the form of raised tuffets or scratches which can deflect the ball. These must *not* be repaired and you should take care not to flatten them either by walking along the line of your putt or in the course of repairing a pitch mark. One often sees golfers mend a pitch mark by jabbing at it with a tee peg or repair tool and then flattening the area by pressing down on it with a foot. That practice is not illegal in itself but the act of standing on the pitch mark may incidentally flatten a spike mark. It is much better to get into the safe and sound golfing habit of repairing pitch marks by gently raising the depressed area with a tee peg or repair fork and then lightly flattening the surface with the sole of your putter. Do not tamp it down hard; just allow the natural weight of the putter to smooth out the irregularities.

IMPEDIMENTS
You are also allowed to remove loose impediments from the line of your putt. These may include fallen leaves, worm-casts, sand thrown onto the green from a bunker, loose earth, snow and ice. Once again you must take great care in how you proceed in moving impediments. There is a general prohibition against improving your line as well as a specific ban on testing the surface of the green. Wholesale sweeping operations along the line of your putt would thus constitute a double infringement. One reason why golfers would like to test the surface is to discover the direction of the grain, or nap. Grass seldom grows straight upwards like the bristles on a hair brush but tends to grow in one direction. This grain is particularly pronounced on courses which are in the hotter latitudes and while the rule of thumb has it that the grass grows towards the direction of the setting sun, it often happens that one green will have areas of grain in quite contrary directions.

The influence of grain on the roll of a ball can be uncannily powerful and it is common in places such as South Africa and the southern USA to watch your putt apparently defy the laws of gravity and veer *up* what is patently a *down*slope. So you need to know how the grain lies but you must not test the surface. The answer is to use your eyes. When the grain lies away from you, the grass has a glossy sheen while it appears dull and matt when the grain is towards you. Some tournament professionals actually map the grain for every green during their practice rounds in case the competition days should happen to be overcast, when 'reading the nap' becomes more difficult. So be wary about the way you brush aside loose impediments and save yourself the risk of an accusation of testing the surface. A light sweeping motion with the back of the hand or putter head is recommended.

TOUCHING THE LINE
Another preliminary to putting to which you are entitled is the advice of your partner or caddie on the correct line, if only to confirm your own judgement. Former Open Champion Max Faulkner had a caddie who used to study the line of a putt through a pair of opera glasses from which the lenses had long since vanished and then invariably produced the advice: 'Hit it slightly straight, sir.' If you do take advice, make sure that your caddie or partner does not touch the surface of the green (9). That is illegal so the rule is 'Point, don't touch' or, better still, an oral suggestion such as 'Two inches outside the right lip.'

FLAGSTICKS (34)
You are now ready to putt and you have to decide what you would like to have done with the flagstick: taken out, attended, or held up. It is a two shot penalty or loss of hole if your putt (from on the green, of course) hits the flagstick, so if you decide to have it attended, be sure that the person on the flagstick knows that it must be removed before your ball reaches the hole. This is one of the commonest sources of mishap since the flagstick may jam in the hole and resist all the tugging of the attendant. When you are attending the flagstick for someone else, take the precaution of easing it so that it will come out smoothly, and if it is a windy day it is a usual courtesy to gather the folds of the actual flag in your hand, so that its flapping will not distract the person putting. On sunny days make sure you stand so that your shadow does not fall across the hole on the line of the putt.

Advocates of simplified golf rules find much ammunition in the complexities of the regulations covering the flagstick. Many of the rules do seem entirely superfluous to the essence of golf and merely achieve the highly undesirable effect of slowing the already tedious process of putting ever further. However, the rules exist and must be observed, so let us quickly run through the fine print. As we have seen, you may elect, before making your stroke, to have the flagstick attended, removed or held up. If you have been unwise enough to leave the flagstick in the hole, once your ball has been struck you cannot shout 'Take it out!' On the green we all tend to become slightly preoccupied by the task in hand and often an opponent, or fellow competitor, or caddie, will automatically attend the flag. If this is done with your knowledge, and you make no objection, then you are assumed to have authorised it. However, if it is done *without* your knowledge or authority, and you should then hit the flagstick or the attendant with your ball, there is no penalty. You play the ball as it lies. Finally, there are the occasions when you play from off the green and your ball lodges agonisingly against the flagstick, suspended above the hole but without dropping. Now you may have the flagstick removed – best to do the job yourself, with great care – and if the ball drops then you have holed out with your last shot.

CROQUET PUTTING (35)
In making your actual stroke, remember that croquet putting has been banned. That is, you must not stand astride a line extending from the hole through your ball. Many golfers were dismayed when croquet putting was outlawed because the method certainly enabled them to make a decent stroke after their nerves had long since rendered orthodox putting ineffective. On balance, however, croquet putting was foreign to the traditions of golf and while the ban may have been hard on certain individuals, it did at least preserve golfing orthodoxy. If you find that putting is much easier when you have two eyes facing directly at the hole, then try the style adopted by Sam Snead. He faces the hole and putts with the ball alongside his right foot, steadying the top of his putter with the left hand and swinging the club with a pushing movement of his right hand held down the shaft.

BALL OVERHANGING HOLE (35)
It often happens that your putt will run right to the lip of the hole and then stop, greatly to your chagrin. In that case, the rules allow you to wait a 'few seconds' only for the putt to drop. You must not dance around the hole, or blow at the ball in your frustration (as once happened in a competition) or stand like a statue in the hope that the ball will finally topple over the brink. What you should do is walk to the hole and then let your conscience count off 'a few seconds'. There is still an outside chance that a puff of wind might budge it and while you are no longer at liberty just to stand there, you are perfectly entitled to begin to take up a proper address position for the *coup de*

Remember that croquet putting has been banned, but if you find that putting is much easier when you have two eyes facing directly at the hole, then try the style adopted by Sam Snead.

grâce. That gives you another moment of hope for if the ball drops *before* you have addressed it (and, remember, that means taking your stance and grounding your putter behind the ball) then you are considered to have holed out with your previous putt. But if it drops after you have addressed it, even if you have not taken the club-head back, then you are ruled to have caused the ball to move and it counts as another putt.

Your responsibilities on the green do not end when you hole out. You have an obligation to show due courtesy to others while they putt. That means standing still, well out of their area of vision, and keeping quiet.

MARKING THE BALL (35)

Now for the troublesome business of when to mark your ball and what happens if your ball accidentally hits someone else's. The normal rule of golf applies that the ball furthest from the hole is to be played first and in stroke-play if there is another competitor's ball remotely near the line of your putt you may ask him to mark and lift it. In practice, most players usually mark and lift their balls automatically, in order to clean them, and only replace them when it is their turn to putt. If you fail to take these elementary precautions, which ought to become a matter of habit, and your ball hits a fellow competitor's, then you incur a two stroke penalty. The other player's ball must immediately be replaced in its original position.

In match-play, you still have the right to ask your opponent to mark his ball but there will be times when you feel it is to your advantage to have it left on the green. If it lies alongside the hole, for instance, your ball may be deflected into the cup. There is no penalty if your ball hits his and your opponent has the option of replacing his ball on its original spot or leaving it in its new position. Beware of this practice of leaving an opponent's ball near the hole in the hope of a lucky rebound. Nearly every large match-play tournament produces one example of this ploy backfiring. Instead of rebounding into the hole, the ball knocks the opponent's ball into the cup and he is then considered to have holed out with his previous putt.

The rules of golf do not specify any standard procedure for marking the position of your ball but certain guidelines laid down by the professional bodies for tournament golf have been so widely followed as to have acquired the status of normal golfing conventions. The marking of the ball is one of the favourite areas for that tiny minority of rogues who are looking for ille-

If you mark your ball with the marker nearer the hole, and then replace your ball on the other side of the marker, you will very soon get the reputation of a highly suspicious character.

gal advantage and there was one professional who was notorious for his sly attempts to cheat. He was finally cured of his unorthodox sleight of hand with a ball marker during the British Professional Match-play Championship when his opponent announced curtly: 'Mark your ball again and I'll give you the putt.' It was in order to eliminate that kind of behaviour, or even the suspicion of it, that the professionals' associations introduced instructions for the proper marking of a ball on the green. Using a small coin, or a regular ball-marker specially made for the purpose, you should place it as close to the ball as possible, pressing it firmly into the turf at the point furthest from the hole. In other words, you line up the hole, ball and marker and when you come to replace the ball by its marker it will be returned to its original position with no possibility of having gained an iota of advantage. (One common method of cheating is to mark the ball with the marker between ball and hole and then to replace the ball in front of the marker, thus 'stealing' a fractional, if helpful, advantage.) It may be that your opponent or fellow competitor asks you to move your marker to one side as it might interfere with the roll of his putt. In that case you proceed as above, marking and lifting the ball, and then measure on a club-head's width (or two, as requested) to the side, as near as possible to a right-angle to the line between your marker and the hole. When you replace the ball you first measure back the width of a club-head, move the marker, put down the ball and then lift the marker. If you cannot trust yourself accurately to judge a right-angle when moving the marker to one side, you can easily take a fix on some landmark such as a tree or fence post to fix the positions. What you do not do in these cases is to measure off one club-head's width from the ball itself and then mark the other end of the putter head. That way is sloppy and open to abuse. By the same token, it is bad form to mark your ball by planting a tee-peg alongside it, since you may raise a spike mark in removing the peg, and it is no less than petty vandalism to mark the ball by scoring the turf with the point of a tee peg.

CONCESSIONS

In match-play, if you wish to concede your opponent a putt without requiring him to hole out, there are two points to be borne in mind. Firstly, it is essential to make the concession in absolutely unambiguous terms. If he puts up close and you say 'That's good' it could be taken as a compliment on his skill or as an expression of conceding the next putt. Strictly speaking, you should remove his ball and hand it to him as a formal act of concession, but that is not always convenient if you are standing yards away waiting to make your putt. So, if you concede verbally, say so in unequivocal terms and then there can be no confusion.

The other point about these concessions is to eliminate all feeling of guilt. The man who bridles because he has not been conceded a 12 in. putt is half way to being beaten, specially if he allows his resentment to simmer on until the next tee. He will surely hit a bad drive because an angry golfer is a bad golfer. It is a sound idea to discipline yourself never to anticipate a concession and, consequently, never to feel disappointment when it does not come. Eliminate all thoughts of so-called sportsmanship in this area. There is nothing sporting about wanting to see a short putt holed out and so if you putt up close to the hole, go straight to your ball and mark it. Your opponent will tell you if he wants it left where it is. That way, you will be mentally preparing yourself for the short one and will be more likely to hole it if necessary. If you never expect a concession you will never lose your mental equilibrium.

BALL ON THE WRONG GREEN

On occasions your ball will land on a green other than the one to which you were playing. By now you will have realised that the spirit and customs of golf are opposed to golfers digging divots out of pristine putting surfaces with deep-soled pitching wedges. The rules of golf have anticipated your dilemma. In this event you must lift your ball and drop it without penalty off the green, as near as possible to where it lay but not nearer the hole and not into a hazard.

CASUAL WATER

As for the other eventualities which may arise on the green, the commonest is casual water (including snow and ice) but you can also meet examples of ground under repair (properly marked) and holes and scrapes made by burrowing animals. In this instance the condition does not have to affect the lie of the ball or your stance but may be anywhere on a line between your ball – provided it is on the green – and the hole. If so, you may lift your ball without penalty and *place* it in the nearest position which provides maximum relief. If your ball is off the green you get no relief from such conditions intervening on the green. The reason for stressing that word 'place' is to underline the fact that a ball is never dropped on a green. If you have lawful occasion to lift and move your ball you may tee it up if on a teeing ground, you must drop it through the green – and that includes fairways, rough and hazards – and you must place it on the green.

7 RIGHTS AND DUTIES

*Marking the card — Know and use the rules — The golfer's rights —
Amateur status*

MARKING THE CARD (38, 39)

In April 1968 an estimated twenty million people watching the live telecast of the climax of the US Masters saw Roberto de Vicenzo get down in three strokes on the 17th hole. That birdie was enough to put the popular Argentinian in a tie with Bob Goalby. There would have to be a play-off in the morning to settle the issue. Roberto walked off the last green to a standing ovation which was as much a tribute to his outstanding sportsmanship and skill over his distinguished career as to his play in this final round. At the age of 45, Roberto was running out of time if he was to add the green jacket of the Masters champion to his British Open Championship medal. No man, save possibly Sam Snead, had won more tournaments (neither had a clear idea of how many victories they had achieved) but the classics had largely escaped Roberto. Here was his chance and it was a moment of high emotion as he signed his card and handed it to the recorder. Then came the bombshell. It was announced that Roberto had signed an incorrect card. The total was correct but the figures did not tally because the marker, Tommy Aaron, had inadvertently entered a 4 opposite the 17th hole. The rule admitted no possibility of a loop-hole; it stated unequivocally that if a player signed for a score lower than his actual score he must be disqualified. And if he signed for a higher score than his actual score (as in this case) then that score must stand. It did not make any difference that eye witnesses by the thousand were prepared to swear to that birdie. (Actually, their testimony would not have been conclusive since it is possible that if, say, Roberto's ball had moved at the address, only he and his marker would have known about it.) Nor could there be any special dispensation under the rule of equity; the rules did not admit that possibility. It was quite clear that the spurious 4 would have to stand, as attested by the signatures of player and marker.

There were plenty of precedents, including the equally tragic case of Mrs Jackie Pung, whose cup of triumph in the 1957 US Women's Open was dashed from her lips in identical fashion. So the green blazer was ceremoniously presented to Bob Goalby. It proved to be a hollow victory. Instead of winning the universal plaudits which he had legitimately earned, he was widely regarded as the man who took the Masters by default. That feeling, totally unfair to Goalby, who was bitterly disappointed that he could not play off with Roberto for an unambiguous decision, cost him thousands of dollars from commercial endorsements. We can never say that the mistake by the marker cost Roberto the Masters – and for two reasons. Firstly, and obviously, no one can assert what the outcome of the play-off might have been. Secondly, and more importantly, the responsibility for returning an accurate card rests squarely on the player.

The marker's job is to check the score with the competitor for each hole and record it. But the competitor himself is solely responsible for the correctness of the card which he signs. No alterations can be made to a card after it has been signed and handed in to the committee. As a matter of incidental interest, the Roberto de Vicenzo affair persuaded the Masters committee to institute the procedure of having competitors go to a special tent behind the 18th green where they can sit quietly, compose their emotions and calmly check their cards before signing them. Any doubtful points can be cleared up at this time.

What exactly is the information which a competitor is required to provide on his card before he adds his signature? Well, in club events, which is the highest form of competitive golf to which most of us aspire, the player has a duty before starting play to see that the card issued to him by the committee has marked on it his name and his current handicap. Make sure those details are correct before you hit a ball because if you play off a higher handicap than your current one, you will be disqualified. And if you play off a lower handicap than your correct one then the score stands off that lower handicap. As for the other entries on the card, the rules make only one requirement – that the gross score for each hole shall be entered in the appropriate spaces. You are not required to work out your net scores, nor add up the totals or points. That is up to the committeemen and if you try to do their job for them you risk making a mistake which cannot be rectified later. Every year in professional tournaments some poor golfer comes to grief through entering totals. What usually happens is that the marker inadvertently enters the total for the first nine holes in the space for the ninth hole. The total is correct enough and that is what the player confirms when he signs his card. But now the committee sees a figure of 36 entered for the ninth hole. And, as we have seen, that is the score which the rules insist must be accepted. So instead of a 72, the player finds himself credited with 104 and he is out of the tournament. So always double-check the scores for individual holes; it does not matter if you make an error in the adding-up or handicap conversions. Do not sign your card and leave your marker to hand it in to the committee. There have been cases of markers forgetting to hand in cards until it was too late. It is the player's duty to hand in his own card, signed and countersigned, as soon as possible after completion of his round.

KNOW AND USE THE RULES (37)
Another important responsibility which the rules place on every competitor is that he should make himself familiar with the rules and conditions of the competition. You should also have with you copies of the rules and local rules. That may sound so fundamental as to be unnecessary but it is surprising how many golfers enter a competition with only the haziest ideas of what it is all about. You hear them on the first tee asking which tee-markers they should be using or whether winter rules are in force. Committees have wide powers to bring in local rules to cover abnormal conditions (such as excessive mud), the preservation of the course (which could mean a ban on playing off ground under repair in a recently seeded area) and allowing special relief from roads, paths or drainage trenches. In addition, the committee has a duty to provide clear definitions of water hazards, ground under repair, out of bounds, obstructions and integral parts of the course. You should take a close look at the local and competition rules before starting and it is as well to get into the habit, after putting out on each green, to consult the local rules for any special conditions governing the next hole. The strategy of your play may very well be influenced by prior knowledge of unsuspected out of bounds, or suchlike. That information should be printed on the card. Temporary local rules are usually displayed only on the club notice board. If winter rules are in force, pay particular attention to the details as such rules are liable to vary from course to course. On some occasions you may

be permitted to lift, clean and place within 6 in. of your original lie on the fairway, not nearer the hole, and at other times the rule might be to 'roll' the ball within a club's length, not nearer the hole. Sometimes relief in wet conditions applies only to a ball which is plugged in its own pitch marks. Mark well whether the local rules provide for such balls to be dropped or placed, cleaned or not, and whether the provision covers 'fairway' or 'through the green'. The Rules of Golf do not acknowledge any distinction between 'fairway', 'rough' and 'semi-rough' – all these conditions being blanketed together in the expression 'through the green'. But local rules may specify 'fairway' and you should make a point of getting the local rule clear in your mind before playing.

Before we leave the subject of 'through the green', we may as well clear up a common misconception. There is an idea abroad among many golfers that 'rough' must be regarded as a 'hazard' in applying the rules. In other words, if you have a free drop in a bunker, you must always drop within the bunker (22), so if in rough, you must always drop in the rough. That is not the case at all. If your ball is in, say, casual water in the edge of the rough it may well be that you can legitimately drop out on the fairway. That is your good luck and you should take it. On the other hand, there will be occasions when you will have to drop from the fairway into the rough and you must accept those bad rubs of the green along with the good.

THE GOLFER'S RIGHTS
By this stage it is hoped that you have absorbed a solid grounding in the main rules of golf but that does not mean that you will never have to consult the official rule book. You certainly will, and a copy of the rules should be a permanent accessory in your golf bag. (Keep this book in a plastic bag so that it does not get soggy in rainy weather.) There are one or two useful hints on how to consult the book.

The first thing to do is to think in the precise, legal terms which the rules employ. That is to say, of a 'flagstick' and not 'pin' or 'stick'; 'bunker', not 'trap'; 'stroke-play', not 'medal-golf'. Distinguish clearly between the rules of match-play and stroke-play. You will find the appropriate rule from the comprehensive index and before forming a decision scrutinise the definitions to confirm that the rule applies to your exact situation. In complex cases, where more than one rule may be involved, take the sequence step by step.

Distinguish between a 'ball in play', a 'provisional ball', an 'alternate ball' and 'ball out of play'. At any time during the round your ball may be any of these and even an outside agency. Take the example of a player in stroke-play who tees up outside the teeing-ground and then drives out of bounds. Is he penalised for both infringements? The answer is No. A ball played from outside the teeing-ground is not 'in play' and therefore the fact that it goes out of bounds is irrelevant. The only penalty is for playing from outside the teeing ground.

Sometimes the sheer complexity of the incident will defy all attempts to extract an acceptable decision from the rules. Always remember that in stroke-play you have the option of playing an alternate ball and then letting the committee unscramble the legal niceties later. Be sure to raise the query before you sign the card. In match-play you and your opponent have to come to an agreement before moving on to the next hole. In most cases, when the natural justice of the situation so suggests, you can shelve the problem by mutually agreeing on a half.

Your attitude to the rules is all important. Accept your due penalties with good grace. Fretting about your bad luck will only make matters worse because it will distract your concentration for subsequent shots. But remember that the rules can also help you on many occasions and it may be helpful to review some of the elements in what might be called the golfer's Bill of Rights.

You have the right to

Re-tee your ball whenever you have reason to return to the teeing-ground to play another ball (29).

Re-tee your ball if it falls off the peg before you make your stroke (14).

Recall an opponent's shot played from outside the teeing ground (44).

Recall an opponent's shot played out of turn from the teeing-ground (13).

A free drop from ground under repair (including piled grass cuttings), scrapes made by burrowing animals and casual water (32).

Remove loose impediments, except in a hazard (18).

Remember that the rules can also help you. A decision makes it clear that a golfer should not put himself into physical danger. In this case he should drop another ball in a safe place not nearer the hole.

Remove movable obstructions anywhere, and to replace your ball without penalty if it moves during the removal of an obstacle (31).

A free drop from immovable obstructions (31).

Ascertain from your opponent the number of strokes he has taken at any time (10).

Replace a ball which becomes unfit for play (28)

Another drop, without penalty, if you accidentally drop in a wrong place (22).

Ask anyone for information about the line of play through the green, or about the position of the flagstick (9).

Make practice swings at any time and to play practice strokes (except in hazards) between the play of two holes, provided you do not play on or to any green except the one just played (8 note 1).

Replace any club which becomes unfit in normal play and to bring your total complement up to fourteen clubs (3).

In stroke-play to put an alternative ball into play in disputed situations (11).

The lie which your shot gave you (16).

Lift your ball to identify it (23).

Search for five minutes for a lost ball (def 6).

Refrain from grounding your club in precarious rough or on the green in windy conditions, so that if your ball moves after you have taken your stance you are not penalised (27f).

Clean your ball before every stroke on the green (35).

Repair pitch marks on the green (35).

Replace the ball if yours is moved by an outside agency (27).

Clean your ball when taking relief under the rules (23).

Suspend play if you feel threatened by lightning or fall ill (37).

Take equitable evasive action for relief from physical danger (26).

Seek and accept advice from your partner or either of your caddies (9).

A free drop in a hazard if your ball is lost in casual water, scrapes made by burrowing animals or ground under repair in that bunker (32).

Touch grass or banking materials on your backswing when playing from a bunker (33).

There are many more rights which could be distilled from the rules, but this list will possible serve to demonstrate that the laws can and should be used in a positive way and not be seen purely as a catechism of prohibitions and penalties.

AMATEUR STATUS
The government of golf is shared between the Royal and Ancient Golf Club of St Andrews, Scotland, and the United States Golf Association. These two bodies maintain a close liaison and meet formally from time to time to consider revisions in the rules. All national associations are affiliated to one or other of the two parent organisations and are consulted before changes are introduced. In theory the government of golf may appear to be autocratic but the way it works in practice, with extensive interchange of views on an unofficial basis among all the golfing nations, is democratic enough. Proof of that assertion is to be found in the undoubted fact that golf passes the ultimate test of democracy, in that its government is conducted by the consent of the vast majority of golfers.

By and large the rules of the R and A conform exactly with those of the USGA. One major exception is the size of the ball – not less than $1 \cdot 68$in in diameter in countries under USGA jurisdiction and not less than $1 \cdot 62$in in diameter in the R and A code. Thus the bigger ball is perfectly legal all over the world but the smaller ball is not permitted in competition in areas where the USGA writ is in force.

Another area of divergence is the matter of amateur status. The value of a prize which an amateur may receive without jeopardising his amateur status varies slightly, although the difference is more apparent than real. We golfers are expected, even obliged, to ensure that we do not accept a prize whose retail value exceeds the limit of $250 or £100, according to where the competition was held. In fact, that is an intolerable responsibility. What prize-winner would have the gall, or the knowledge, to challenge the value of his prize and reject it? Nobody. We have to take on trust that a competition run according to the rules of golf is conforming to the legal limits on prizes.

In general the rules of amateur status have been framed to prevent the very best amateur players from exploiting their skill and fame for personal gain and so for 99 out of 100 golfers there is no call for a thorough knowledge of the regulations. After all, the average golfer is unlikely to be paid to teach golf, or allow his name to be used in advertising, or make personal appearances, or sell golf equipment, or to be offered privileges or expenses to play golf. We are mostly very small fish in the golfing ocean and the nets of amateur status are designed to catch only the big sharks. The one regulation which applies to everyone is the rule against *any conduct, including activities in connection with golf gambling, which is considered detrimental to the best interests of the game.*

This rule is so sweeping in its implications that it could be invoked to cover almost any eventuality, from having one drink too many in the club bar to deliberately raising one's handicap. In practice this rule is not operated as a broad threat looming over golfers to be of good behaviour at all times. The ruling bodies do not police the game to keep its adherents on the straight-and-narrow path of righteousness. Indeed, our golfing Big Brothers do not care what we get up to provided we do not break the cardinal rule, which operates in golf just as it does in life. We must not be caught. Once our transgressions get our names into the newspapers, or create a scandal, and the good name of golf is put at risk, then – and with reluctance – Big Brother feels forced to take action. Then, the ultimate sanction is a formal notification that we have forfeited our amateur status. So what? How does that affect the average man in the street who enjoys a couple of games of golf at the weekend? In fact, the punishment can prove to be quite severe. The miscreant is thrust into a golfing limbo in which he is neither a pro nor an amateur. If he is a member of a golf club he will have to put his case to the committee. The club might decide that he could not remain a member. He would certainly not be allowed to enter competitions as an amateur, except possibly those limited to members of his club and only then with the express permission of the club. So it could well be that loss of amateur status could deprive a golfer of all the sociability of club life which makes up such a large proportion of the enjoyment of the game. He could be confined to green-fee golf, playing at municipal courses or any clubs willing to accept him. And the process of reinstatement as an amateur, after a probationary period of exemplary amateur conduct, can be a long and tedious business.

Amateurism is not a subject over which we golfers need lose much sleep. The whole concept of amateurism at this point in history is outdated and the very word has come to mean something quite different from that originally intended. Today when we speak of 'amateur' we use the term pejoratively to convey a feeling of second-rate or incompetent. The amateur in the modern sense is not so much a man who is not paid but one who does not deserve pay. That view is gaining slow acceptance within golf and is expressed in that process of discussion and informal pressure which motivates the custodians of the rules. However, the process of legal reform in golf grinds exceedingly slowly. Perhaps one day the rules will be changed to take account of modern social conditions, recognising that the day of the independently wealthy golfer who could play the game as a true amateur is past. In the meantime, the rules remain and we must all pay lip service to them, if only to the extent of following the dictum: 'Do not get caught.'

8 COURSE BEHAVIOUR

Practice swings — Undue delay — Unseen and unheard — Rule of the road — On the green

Every copy of the Rules of Golf is prefaced by a section headed 'Etiquette'. That archaic word, which reeks of the social rituals of Victorian snobbery, is enough to switch off anyone in this egalitarian age. Golf retains this hangover from the past out of respect for tradition, which is a worthy enough motive. But by preserving the word 'etiquette' the rulers of golf are actually nourishing the shadow of tradition while neglecting the substance of that tradition, which is the established code of good golfing behaviour. Retaining the word etiquette is counter-productive, since it offends the free spirit of contemporary golfers and puts them in quite the wrong frame of mind to accept the timeless advice under that antiquated heading. It is rather like a winemaker refusing to change his labels even though the name of his product has changed in popular usage over the years and has come to be synonymous with 'poison'. The contents may be as good as ever but it makes for problems in marketing. The custodians of golf traditions would hardly try to sell their code of golfing manners under the heading 'Snobbish mumbo-jumbo evolved by toffs to distinguish themselves from riff-raff like you and me' but that is more or less what etiquette has come to mean in the minds of most of us. So let us steam the label off the bottle and sample the contents with an open mind.

Even so, we still have to combat a certain amount of consumer resistance. Nobody likes to be lectured on how to behave. Who do these people think they are, patronising us with their rules of conduct? We already know how to behave, off the golf course or on it. The reaction may be natural but, sadly, it is not entirely valid when it comes to golf. At least, that is how it works out in practice. Theoretically, as we read the strictures on golfing behaviour in the tranquillity of our homes, we accept absolutely the words: *No player should play until the players in front are out of range.* What could be more obvious? Who among us would deliberately seek to maim a fellow golfer? The reminder seems superfluous. Yet every day golfers are injured by drives raining down on them from behind. It is not that the act of picking up a golf club turns a man into a homicidal maniac; it is simply that on the golf course we all become so bound up in our problems, and concentrate so fiercely – as the instruction books exhort us – that we tend to be oblivious of anything else. This total preoccupation is the real justification for a written code of behaviour. Just as we have to discipline our minds to think about the rules as we play, so we must make a positive effort to spare a thought for other players on the course. What could be more natural, on sinking a long putt, than to give vent to a whoop of delight? It is simply a harmless expression of joy. Harmless? Possibly not. Just behind the trees there may be another green, and another golfer setting himself to an equally important putt. As he takes his club back your scream of delight pierces his envelope of concentration like an electric shock. He reacts with a reflex convulsion and, in his anger, probably misses the one back. His day is spoiled.

All the rules of behaviour are based on consideration for others. And since golf is such a private activity, in essence, it is all too easy to forget about other people. That is why we all have to work on cultivating good habits so that they become second nature. Our natural instincts of consideration for other people may well become submerged in the heat of golfing battle, so we must ingrain them.

PRACTICE SWINGS
Many of the canons of behaviour have been touched upon in earlier chapters but it will do no harm to take another look at the commoner conventions and analyse the reasons for them. One of the most important concerns the practice swing. We are all perfectionists and so the commonest subject of concern in the golfer's mind as he tramps around the course is how to improve on that last shot. The urge to swing a club and get the feel of a pure stroke which will eliminate that dreadful slice, or hook, is overwhelming. We know we can do it. A couple of practice swings will put everything right. Nothing else matters. Well, one thing that certainly does matter is that fellow just over there who is about to play his shot. Our flailing away at the empty air is a distraction even if we are quite far away, a fact of which we

become painfully aware when it is our turn to play and we are the victim of a human windmill out of the corner of our eye. In fact, a practice swing is of dubious benefit, except to loosen the muscles before a round. Civilised life conditions us all to abhor desecration of turf. The gardeners among us sweat to produce beautiful lawns. Public notices exhort us to keep off the grass. Subconsciously or consciously, we hate to destroy grass. Of course, if there is a golf ball sitting on it, then that is quite a different matter. That hypnotic white sphere eliminates every instinct except the desire to bash the thing a quarter of a mile. But without a ball, when the strike area is virgin turf, the natural tendency is to preserve it. The daisy is a weed, though, and there is no restraint on knocking its head off. So that becomes the target. A perfect practice swing flows through the summer air and the daisy is neatly decapitated. Now, with our muscle-memory refreshed on the execution of the perfect swing, we are ready for the ball. However, the swing that kills a daisy will – if we reproduce it exactly – catch a golf ball a glancing blow on the head. In short, the practice swing may well be the sure guarantee of a bad golf shot. The answer, you may think, is to hit down into the turf with the practice swing, and gouge out a chunk of mother earth. Well that will not make us popular with the greens committee if we indulge the habit to excess. A reasonable amount of vandalism of turf is acceptable in practice swinging provided the divots are replaced although the habit should be severely restricted on the tee, particularly on the tees of short holes where iron shots are played. Greens committees have a problem maintaining teeing grounds and their job is made much more difficult if we indulge in wholesale ploughing operations with excessive practice swings. And on tees divots should not be replaced. The reason for this anomaly is that a replaced divot can provide an unstable platform from which to hit a golf ball. The ball may move just as the club-head is coming down – and that means a muffed shot for certain. If the ball is on a peg it may fall off and, as we have seen, if the downswing has begun when this happens it counts as a shot even if the club-head fails to make contact.

UNDUE DELAY
Novice golfers quickly learn that the 'correct' drill when someone else is playing a shot is to stand opposite him, clear of his range of vision and not to fidget, or make a noise. Actually, this is the procedure for a *caddie*. It would

be a time-wasting ritual for players to take up this position. All that is necessary is to ensure that we are well out of the way, out of sight and out of mind of the person who is playing his shot. If he does not like having anyone behind him he is at liberty to ask us politely to move. And provided we are well out of the way there is no need to stand like a statue, with eye riveted on the player and all ready to call 'Good shot' or 'Bad luck.' There is no call for us to provide an audience for every shot. Indeed, it is often a sound policy not to watch the laboured gyrations of partners and opponents. Our own impeccable swings may become infected by the parodies of style and tempo which we observe. The only duty we have – and it is an important one, although much neglected – is to watch the flight of another player's ball so that we can give an accurate answer to his anguished question: 'Where did that one go?' For the rest, we can better spend the time while he is waggling in pondering on the initial calculations for our own shots. That way, we will be ready, once his ball is on the way, to whip out a club and let fly. Slow play is the bane of modern golf and one of the major reasons for it – we will come to more in a moment – is the time-wasting convention of switching off all thoughts of our own games while others play, and then only getting down to the job in hand when all the rest of our group are arranged into a motionless and silently admiring audience. If four players are ranged in line across a wide fairway there is no earthly reason why each of them should not be calculating the shot, selecting a club and taking up a stance more or less simultaneously. The setting up of a golf shot can be as ponderous as the loading of a Roman siege catapult, with interminable adjustments to range and aim before finally the carcass of a dead horse is hoisted into the missile-launcher. Lobbing four dead horses over the parapet takes an age, which is how it works in golf if three crews of loaders and launchers sit down and watch while the fourth goes into action. In this kind of situation the golf balls should fly into the green more as a ragged salvo. This applies even more strongly on the green, where we commonly see three players standing politely and patiently in a group at the edge of the green while the fourth player goes through his tediously mystic ritual of marking, cleaning and replacing his ball, observing the line of his putt from all four cardinal points of the compass, peering into the hole (presumably to ascertain if the aperture is large enough to accommodate a golf ball), squinting at his putter while he holds it at arm's length with finger and thumb as if it were an unexploded bomb, indulging in a lengthy series of practice swings and then shuffling interminably at the address before finally making his stroke. The process takes up to two minutes, although that is by no means a record, and by the time the short ones have been lifted and cleaned and tapped home, it is common for a four-ball to spend 10 minutes on one green.

The entire process can be streamlined if everyone does his preliminary thinking simultaneously and mentally prepares himself to step up to his putt and hit it, as soon as it is his turn. Some golfers may argue that good putting demands thorough reconnaissance and a leisurely execution. If true, then it is true only up to a point. There is clearly a limit beyond which extra fussing and fuming and fiddling actually reduces the chance of success. Some of the best putters are brisk and businesslike. Besides, there are two positive advantages in the habit of stationing yourself behind your own ball and surveying the line while another player is putting out: you eliminate watching him putt – few human activities are more tedious – and by speeding up the match you ensure more time in the club-house after the game.

UNSEEN AND UNHEARD
It may sound a counsel of perfection, but expletives are best deleted on the golf course, specially when playing with strangers. There are still people in these permissive days who are offended by swearing and even if we are among friends the sheer volume of our curse may carry to a neighbouring match and put somebody off his stroke. Anger, like joy, is best expressed *sotto voce*. The one time it is permitted, nay obligatory, to turn up the volume is when a wayward shot looks as if it might hit somebody, or even land near him. Then a warning shout of 'Fore!' is entirely in order, since a ruined golf shot is a fate less severe than a smack on the back of the head from a ball travelling at more than 100 mph.

In essence, the conventions of golfing conduct add up to an ideal which would make it appear after our round that we had never even set foot on the course. All our divots have been invisibly mended; our footprints have been meticulously smoothed from the bunkers; no witness can be found who was on the course at the time who heard us or even, hopefully, who saw us. They were all so preoccupied in their own enjoyment that even if we came into their view we did not register on the memory. The reality is all too often far short of that ideal. An excursion round a golf course is all too often

Your harmless expression of joy (like the player's, background left) may spoil someone else's day.

like following in the wake of a particularly undisciplined army fleeing from battle. Discarded equipment in the form of beer cans, cigarette packets and ball-wrappers litter the grass; footprints trace the progress of the rabble through the bunkers; pitch marks pock-mark the greens like Lilliputian shell craters. The culprits have affected the enjoyment of our game. The least we can do is guarantee that we do not leave a similar trail of misery for others.

RULE OF THE ROAD

It is a moot point whether it is more frustrating to be held up on the golf course by slow players ahead, or to be pushed and chivvied by impatient fast players astern. Both situations tend to make us rush our shots and therefore play badly. Certainly more bad blood is created in golf by ignorance of the rule of the road than by any other breach of convention. The word 'ignorance' is selected with some charity, since sheer bloodymindedness is often involved in a refusal to allow a faster match to go through. Normally, two-ball matches have precedence over three- and four-balls and are entitled to go through. A single player has no standing and should give way to all matches. If a match fails to keep its place on the course and loses more than one clear hole on the players in front, it should stand aside and allow the match following to pass. Those rules are quite explicit and should not raise any problems, provided everyone knows the rules. However, there is the delicate question of how to remind the slow players ahead of their duty to give us priority. An ill-tempered shout of 'Fore!' is not the answer since it is tantamount to an accusation of bad manners and is liable to be resented. If we are not invited to go through, the best way is for one of our group to go forward and politely explain that such an invitation would be appreciated. The important element is politeness and a friendly approach. If that fails, then there are no prizes for getting involved in acrimony. Better to endure the discomfort of slow play than to start a dispute which may lead to official reprimands from club officials. A quiet word with the culprits afterwards, or with an official, may prevent future breaches. The one solution to avoid is to despatch a hint in the form of hitting a ball into the sluggardly match ahead. Among some people, as court records testify, this provokes an uncontrollable urge to whack the offending ball back towards its original dispatcher, or out of bounds. Just such a sequence led one golfer to take first umbrage, then a 5-iron from his bag and finally a divot from another player's skull. A knowledge of the rule of the road plus, more importantly, an attitude of consideration for others, could save all that kind of unpleasantness.

A rather more difficult rule to follow is the one which says that any match playing a full round is entitled to pass a match playing a shorter round. The trouble here is that there is no way for the match in front to *know* that those following have priority. Ideally, we should all accept responsibility for calling through matches without any prompting and this means constantly being on the watch for overtaking situations. What frequently happens, of course, is that we are being held up by the match ahead and consequently we assume that it is pointless to call through a quicker match from behind. Maybe. But it is still important to get that message back to the players astern, who may be fuming at our lack of consideration. And if they still want to go through then we should allow them to do so.

The one occasion when it is absolutely essential to call through the following match is when we begin a search for a ball which is clearly not going to be found immediately. That takes precedence over all the rules of priority and two-balls should stand aside for three- and four-balls. In the same way, we should not stand on our right of way. It may be that we are playing an intense singles match of such importance that every shot must be carefully reconnoitred and each individual putt given close and lengthy attention. If we are holding up four players it is inexcusable to ignore the situation and console ourselves with the thought that we have priority. If they are patently playing faster – and they might be playing a foursome, the fastest form of golf, for all we know – then we should call them through. Both matches will benefit from that simple courtesy.

ON THE GREEN
Conduct on the green is even more important, because it is here that a trivial thoughtless action can most easily affect the outcome of the golf, if only because it is here that concentration is fiercest and the condition of the surface is most important. It is not just that an ill-timed cough can cause a putt to be missed; the anticipation of a possible interruption can be just as damaging. Hence, the need to behave at all times with the demeanour of a bishop. A proper sense of reverence should attend our actions, with due consideration for the green and for other players. So . . . the flagstick is removed with care so that the rim of the cup is not damaged. A sharp tug can sometimes dislodge

the liner, which is another reason for the gentle approach. And when attending the flag for another player it is a good idea to ease the flag in its socket, to guarantee that it will come out smoothly. There is nothing more embarrassing than to have it jam, so you are frantically tugging at the thing. If it won't come out and his ball hits it, then he is penalised and will be in no mood to accept apologies. And when attending the flag, make sure that no shadow falls across the line of the putt and on windy days gather the folds of the flag so that its flapping will not be a distraction.

Hold the flag at arm's length to keep footprints as far from the hole as possible; there is nothing quite so maddening as to have your putt deflected from its course by a spike mark close to the edge of the cup. For the same reason, we should never walk on the line of another player's putt and this is not quite as easy as it sounds. Once a player has lifted his ball and replaced it with an almost invisible marker, the position of his line is apt to be forgotten in the preoccupation of the moment. Repairing of pitch marks is a fairly obvious duty (though all too often neglected) and it should be done with due care, lifting the impacted area with a special fork or tee-peg and then smoothing down the repair with the sole of the putter. Simply stamping on the spot, or flattening it with a putter, is not good enough. As to spike marks, we have seen that it is illegal to repair them as you putt. But *after* everyone has putted out and the flag is being carefully replaced it is only considerate to tamp down the worst examples as you move off to the next tee. Damage can also be caused to a green by dropping golf bags on it and by throwing down the flagstick. The convention of leaving golf bags off the green may be taking things rather far, since no damage is done if the thing is placed gently rather than dropped. But it is a safe practice and therefore to be encouraged. In the same way the flagstick should be placed, rather than dropped, and always in a position well clear of any possibility of its being hit by a putt.

When clubs are carried on trolleys or carts the local notices should be strictly observed. It is best always to park *behind* the green and well clear of the fringe. That way players can walk off the back of the green and the players behind can hit their approach shots immediately.

That raises the point about moving off the green without undue delay. There is no doubt that more time is wasted on the green than in any other department of golf. Although the rules allow us to mark and clean a ball for every putt it is not obligatory, even though that impression is sometimes given by pernickety professionals in tournament play. More often than not it is no less than a matter of enlightened self-interest not to clean the ball more than once (if that), as well as being an optional courtesy towards players waiting behind. And when there are people waiting to play into the green it is inexcusable to dawdle about on the green after putting out, by marking cards (better done on the next tee) or chatting, or replaying putts.

In nearly every case, a green is sited close to a tee, which is a thought to be remembered when tempted to emit a yell of delight or anguish at the fate of a putt. Plenty of golfers meticulously hold their peace while the putting is in progress and then launch into an animated post mortem as soon as the flagstick is replaced. Companionable chatter and due expressions of congratulation or commiseration are all part of golf but always subject to the vital proviso that they do not distract other players. Remember the bishop and the due sense of reverence. For many people golf is no less than a secular religion and even if we do not share that degree of obsession we must conduct ourselves as if in a cathedral.

9 COMPETITIONS AND WAGERS

*Bogey and par competitions – Stablefords – Foursomes – Green-
somes – Three-balls and variations – Best ball – Four-ball match-
play – Eclectics – Round Robins – Limited-club competitions –
Pro-ams – Gambling*

Thousands of golfers, notably in America, go through life without ever
deviating from their regular custom of playing straightforward stroke-play.
They have their coterie of special friends and, week in and week out, they
meet to play each other. Their golf takes the form of 'matches' which are decided by a straight comparison of stroke-play scores. The one positive advantage of this custom is that within such a circle of friends the handicaps are
usually mutually adjusted at frequent intervals to guarantee close encounters
and keep the wager money circulating. If that is the way they like it, who are
we to carp? It is none of our business. But the members of such golfing
schools who exist on an unrelieved diet of stroke-play deny themselves the
variety and change of pace offered by some of the different forms of the
game which have survived the test of time. Most clubs organise competitions to cater for the commoner variations and the member who decides
against entering them is denying himself novel golfing experiences and
pleasures which can be obtained in no other way, particularly in foursomes
golf, mixed or otherwise, which produces a whole new range of problems,
anxieties and stresses.

In this chapter we will look at the special rules and conditions covering
these speciality events.

BOGEY AND PAR COMPETITIONS
The term 'bogey' is fast disappearing from all but the most traditional of
clubs and in America the word is now used almost exclusively in its
modern sense to describe a score of one over par for a hole. But it still

lingers on elsewhere in its archaic sense as the target score which should be taken at any hole by a scratch player. It thus differs slightly from 'par' which is defined as the score which a first-class player should take on any hole *in summer conditions*. In most places par is computed on a strictly mathematical basis according to the length of each hole (up to 250 yards, par-3; 251–475 yards, par-4; 476 yards and over, par-5). So when clubs persist with the obsolescent bogey system their cards have separate columns to denote the par rating for each hole and the bogey score (which is usually the same as par except that the longer and more difficult par-4s become bogey-5s). For the sake of simplicity let us forget about bogey and talk only in terms of par competitions. The rules, of course, are identical and the aim is to play a match against an invisible opponent in the form of par. The winner is the player who can finish the most holes up on Old Man Par.

The first pitfall for the uninitiated is that although you are playing a match, hole by hole, this form of golf is played according to the rules of stroke-play. That sounds confusing but is really quite logical. The variations in the rules for match-play are all concerned with the presence of an opponent – what happens if he plays your ball, or if you steal his honour. In a par competition there is no physical enemy, merely a tyrannical figure which you have to equal or beat on each hole. Par cannot intervene in the contest so you are on your own, just as in stroke-play. Therefore you play stroke-play rules. You are allowed three-quarters of your handicap, as in match-play, and your marker is responsible only for recording your gross score at each hole. It is up to the committee to mark the holes at which you receive strokes and to work out your final standing against par. However, you will be well aware of the holes where you get a handicap stroke and once you have played so many shots that it is no longer possible to get even a half against par then you should pick up your ball and leave a blank in the space for that hole's score. The committee will accept such blanks as a loss to par.

STABLEFORDS

In 1931 Dr Frank Stableford of Liverpool invented the Stableford system of scoring and his novel competition proved so enduringly popular that in 1968 this form of golf was given official blessing by being incorporated into the rules of golf. Stablefords are essentially the same as par competitions, using the same stroke-play rules and conventions and with individual competitors usually getting an allowance of seven-eighths of handicap. (This can be varied by the committee and is not governed by a rule of golf.) Remember in computing these allowances that a fraction of a half, or more, counts as a full stroke. Fractions smaller than a half count nothing. Again your only duty is to see that your marker records your gross score for each hole. The committee works out your total on the basis of Dr Stableford's system by awarding one point for every hole completed in a net score of one over par; two points for par; three points for a birdie and so on. The advantage of this method over conventional par and bogey competitions is that it graduates the field more finely. Where a par competition might produce four joint winners all standing three-up on par, their identical scores could well produce an outright winner if their play were computed by Stableford points.

FOURSOMES

Golf is essentially an individual game and the closest it comes to involving the camaraderie and interdependence of team games is in foursomes. For that reason alone – although there are others – it is a pity that many golfers never play foursomes, or Scotch Foursomes as it is commonly known in America. It is commonplace for seasoned professionals and leading amateurs to admit, on being selected for international teams, that this will be their first experience of foursomes. Basically, it is partner golf with each pair playing one ball in alternate strokes. It is officially match-play but this form can also be used in stroke-play or Stablefords. Each partnership decides in advance which of the pair shall drive at the 1st tee. From then on they drive alternately. Thus one player always drives on the odd-numbered holes, his partner at the even, regardless of who may have sunk the last putt on the previous green. During the play of each hole the partners take alternate shots at their joint ball and penalty strokes do not affect this order of play. If a player accidentally plays out of turn – this sometimes happens in the heat of the moment when a player putts up to the lip of the hole and then unthinkingly taps it in – then that stroke is cancelled, the ball is replaced and the side incurs two penalty strokes.

GREENSOMES

Among golfing societies and similar gatherings of like-minded enthusiasts who may have widely varying handicaps, and who may also have indulged themselves freely with cheering spirits over lunch, a popular though unofficial variation on foursomes for a light-hearted afternoon romp is the greensome. The only difference here is that both partners drive at each hole and then select which of their two drives they prefer to play out in alternate shots. A greensome-Stableford is a popular form, with partners receiving three-eighths of the difference in their combined handicaps, just as in foursomes.

THREE-BALLS AND VARIATIONS

We are now getting into deepish water and must be quite sure of our terminology. A three-ball is when three players go out and each man plays a separate match against two separate opponents. Thus there are two distinct matches involved and this type of golf should not be confused with a threesome. This is a match in which a single player competes against a partnership playing alternate shots at the same ball under the same conditions as for foursomes golf.

There are several other variations (unofficial) of enjoyable three-man golf and we might mention two of them. Strictly speaking they are not different forms of golf so much as scoring conventions for the purpose of wagering. Chairman is played to three-ball rules and the first player to win a hole outright is declared to be in the chair. If then, on the next hole, he again wins outright from both opponents he collects the prearranged wager for winning a hole. He remains in the chair if the subsequent hole results in a half with either or both of his opponents but he does not collect any wager. When one of the other two players wins a hole outright he then becomes the new chairman. It can be seen, then, that a player has to win two holes, possibly separated by halves, before he can collect any wager.

The other three-man convention is also match-play and here six points are available on each hole. Perhaps the best way to explain how the points are divided is by example. If B and C both fail to complete a hole then A gets all six points. If A wins a hole, and B and C halve it, then the split is four points to A and one apiece to B and C. If A and B halve, both beating C, then A and B get three points apiece, and C zero. If all halve they get two points each. Finally, if A beats B who in turn beats C, then A gets four points, B two points and C nothing. It sounds rather complicated when put like that but in practice is quite simple and quickly mastered. In order to keep it simple as you go along, and avoid having to keep a written tally of the totals, it is usual after each hole to reduce the lowest score to zero. Thus if A wins the first hole outright from B and C, who halve, the scores would be: $A = 4, B = 1, C = 1$. Now on the second hole A and C halve, both beating B. A and C collect three points apiece so the aggregates now read: $A = 7, B = 1, C = 4$. Reduce poor B's total to zero by subtracting one point all round and proceed to the third tee with the scores at: $A = 6, B = 0, C = 3$. Again it sounds complicated but you soon get the hang of it.

BEST BALL
This is a rare form of match-play golf and is normally used only when a very good player is in the company of two lesser performers. The tiger plays against the better ball of the two rabbits. Best-ball golf can be played against two or three opponents and obviously requires very careful negotiation in the matter of handicapping before any wager is struck. Normally, no handicap allowance is made at all unless the good player is very sure of himself, such as a pro playing against two long-handicap members.

FOUR-BALL MATCH-PLAY
Much commoner is the four-ball match in which partners pit their better ball against the better ball of their opponents. One point to be made about this form of golf is that partners play as a 'side' and this varies the general rule about the ball furthest from the hole to be played first. Here it is the side with a ball furthest from the hole which has the option of selecting which of their two balls is to be played first. There is no penalty through the green, or in a hazard, and no requirement to replay the shot, if a side plays out of turn. On the green, however, if one side plays out of turn the opponents may immediately require the putt to be replayed, in correct order and without penalty. That provision caused much bitterness in the Ryder Cup match at Royal Birkdale in 1969 when the American pair of Ken Still and Dave Hill putted out of turn. They were duly 'called' by their opponents and took umbrage. In the absence of a firm and speedy ruling as to their rights, the Americans conceded the hole in the face of what they considered to be

rulesmanship. The match was played out in high tension and the incident serves to underline the necessity for a sound grasp of the laws and the need to approach disputes with cool detachment. Here the Americans lost a hole which they could have saved by accepting their right to re-putt without penalty.

There are a few other special provisions for this form of golf. Any player can have any ball lifted and if a player's ball moves any other ball in the match, the owner of the moved ball must replace it, without penalty. The most important provision is that if a player's infringement of a rule might help his partner, or adversely affect the other side, then *both* partners incur the relevant penalty. In all other cases an accidental breach of rule does not call down a penalty on the partner. An example may help to clarify this principle. If your ball is deflected by one of your opponents then his side loses the hole, both opponents being penalised because your side was adversely affected. But if you move your ball in lifting a loose impediment, then you suffer the penalty but your partner – who cannot possibly benefit from your action – does not.

Handicapping for four-ball matches is best settled by reducing the lowest handicap player to scratch, thus giving him no strokes. He is called the back marker and this eliminates the absurd possibility of all four players getting a handicap stroke at the same hole. Say the back marker is a 6-handicap player. The rest get three-quarters of the difference between their handicaps and 6. So if a four-ball match consisted of players with handicaps of 6, 12, 16 and 20 the differences would be 0, 6, 10 and 14 and three-quarter allowances would produce 0 strokes, 5 strokes, 8 strokes and 11 strokes (don't forget the fraction rule: half or more counts a stroke, less than a half counts nothing).

ECLECTICS

These are run over a period of time, such as the months of winter, and require a number of stroke-play cards to be returned. Some clubs put no limit on the number of cards which may be returned and this form of competition can produce a useful source of revenue if a separate entry fee is required for each card. At the end of the allotted time the committee sorts through the cards of each competitor and extracts the lowest score returned for each individual hole. It is, incidentally, a great boost to the morale of a veteran club member to work out his lifetime eclectic for his home course. Over a number of years he will have had eagles at most holes, or perhaps better, and quite moderate golfers run up eclectic scores in the low forties. For a man who has never broken 90 on his own course that can be a most comforting thought.

ROUND ROBINS

Unless a club has a really energetic competition secretary, plus good luck, Round Robins tend to be cumbersome and inconclusive affairs. The theory is that each entrant meets everyone else at match-play and the winner is the one who scores most wins. It is a good method of getting the members known to each other but illness and other emergencies can play havoc with the timetable. Provision has to be made for players to concede matches and it is not really satisfactory for a contest to be decided on a number of inevitable concessions.

LIMITED-CLUB COMPETITIONS

A popular novelty which has rather fallen into disuse is the limited-club event. This can take many forms, as the name suggests. A seven-club competition calls for a fair degree of advance planning by the contestants, although not nearly so much preliminary anguish as the competitions in which you are limited to a putter and one other club. The revealing aspect about these events is that the level of scoring is often almost as good as in the club's regular stroke-play competitions. In Europe there is a professional tournament for which the entrants are limited to a 4-iron only. On every occasion on which it has been played the winning score has been below par.

PRO-AMS

Many club golfers are diffident about entering for pro-ams on the grounds that they are not good enough to compete in such illustrious company, possibly watched by scornful spectators, and they are apprehensive about making fools of themselves. The fear may be natural enough, and quite understandable, but it has absolutely no validity so far as the professionals are concerned. Do not be afraid of embarrassing your pro. He does not want to play with the low-handicap tigers. They are no good to him. In most pro-ams three amateurs play off handicap and when any of them produces a better net score than the pro on any hole then that is the score to count.

The 1-handicap player has comparatively little chance of improving on the professional's score. In the natural order of things they will both get par figures on most of the holes. The long-handicap men are the useful partners. You, with your generous stroke allowance, will surely get par figures on some of the holes. And if your handicap strokes fall at those holes you will contribute a birdie every time. So do not be diffident on the basis that you will be no more than a passenger, providing light relief for the others. You will not be that and you will almost certainly benefit your golf from the advice and encouragement of your pro. As for the danger of provoking un-controlled merriment among the crowd, such fears are almost totally illu-sory. As an amateur, people expect you to hit bad shots and once you have exceeded your ration on any hole you can save your blushes by picking up your ball. What is more, as you can console yourself, your bad shots serve to emphasise the skill of your professional. Your black despair is the back-ground against which the diamond of his brilliance is supposed to be con-trasted. In any case, most of the time spectators ignore the laboured efforts of the amateurs and have eyes only for the professionals. So if you get the chance, get out there and enjoy yourself. The only warning which is neces-sary is not to delude yourself before the round that perhaps you will have one of those golden days when everything goes right and you play well above your normal form. That never happens. You always play worse than you thought possible but pro-ams can still be great fun for all that.

GAMBLING
The ruling bodies of golf lay down pious policies on gambling although in their role as custodians of tradition they are on slightly uneasy ground here. Since the earliest recorded minutes of club affairs back in the eighteenth century gambling has played an integral part in golf, to the extent that the clubs maintained 'Bett books'. A special officer was elected to record chal-lenges made at the roisterous club dinners so that there would be written proof when the dawn brought its customary hangover and partial amnesia over the previous evening's bargains. What the legislators really seek to

control is the scope of gambling, rather than the fact of it. There is no doubt that big-money wagers, Calcutta sweepstakes and auction pools can put a severe strain on the ideal of golf as a game of trust and can create suspicion and discord within a club. And as soon as big money becomes involved the spirit of the rules of amateur status is thoroughly compromised. As an amateur you may not accept a golf prize with a retail value of more than £100 or $250 in parts of Europe and areas under the jurisdiction of the United States Golf Association. There is nothing that the authorities can do to stop you having a fat bundle on a private match, which is why they do not even try to prevent it. But as soon as an organised competition is involved, over which the authorities have some control, then they can and do exert a degree of pressure, albeit mostly moral.

You may feel, in passing, that as the winner of a competition you are put into a highly invidious position by your responsibility instantly to appraise the retail value of your prize and then, with as much disdain as you can muster, hand it back if it exceeds the limit. There are steely characters capable of acting with such lofty self-righteousness but for the majority of us frail vessels the euphoria of the occasion, combined with the sheer embarrassment of the alternative, would dull any pricking of conscience. We would, in short, grab the loot and hope the authorities did not get to hear about it. Can we be blamed?

Well, the authorities can and do blame any culprit on whom they can pin a rap. Golfers have been deprived of their amateur status, which thus precludes them from competing in further official competitions. In practice, this is an intolerable responsibility to place on the individual golfer and the authorities would do better to put the onus on competition organisers, over whom they have a measure of control, not to award prizes over the limit.

As for gambling in private golf, nobody cares what you get up to, except possibly your dependants. It is entirely up to you but from a purely golfing point of view it is bad to play for more than you can afford to lose without wincing. That piece of advice might possibly be reversed in the case of young professionals who must learn to play under exceptional stresses; they should always play for a bit more than they can comfortably afford to lose.

For the novice amateur, however, the problem is to work out in advance exactly how high his gambling liability might be. A few of the conventions of golf wagering should be thoroughly absorbed to avoid future distress.

The Nassau is a popular, universal bet. It means that the agreed sum is really trebled. A 'golf-ball Nassau' involves one golf ball on the result of the first nine holes, another ball on the second nine holes and a third ball on the overall result. In four-ball matches the expression 'corner' is much used and frequently misunderstood. It means that the agreed bet is due from both partners, not the joint responsibility of the partnership. Thus if you lose a bet for 'a golf ball a corner' in a four-ball you will be expected to hand over a ball and so will your partner. Just to complicate matters some people use the word 'corner' in the sense of exactly double the above liability. In their terms 'a golf ball a corner' means that both losing partners give a ball apiece to both winners. Since there is no official rule, or definition, it is important to get this situation straightened out before the match. The best plan is to avoid the word 'corner' and agree on the liability for the side. After all, it is just as easy to say 'two golf balls a side'. Then everyone knows exactly what is at stake.

Much more potentially dangerous is the word 'press'. The convention of a press is that a side which becomes two holes down in a match can press their opponents. That starts a secondary bet over the remaining holes and can be followed in due course by yet another press. Simple mathematics shows that a straight bet of one golf ball 'with automatic presses' could cost a side nine balls if the partnership lost every hole. Care is also needed to ensure that everyone understands the same press convention. Some people have a rule that you can only press for half the original stake; others press for the full amount. It could be important for you to know which system you are playing.

If you imagine that it would not be possible to get more complicated than a match with, say, three presses going at once, then you would be vastly mistaken. In four-ball golf it is quite common to have the main partnership bet, with automatic presses, and for all the players to be involved in individual matches with each of the other three players at the same time, again with automatic presses. Now you can be getting into really rich country, even if the basic bet is only one golf ball. Add up the possibilities. Have a really bad day and you could find yourself liable to pay up three-dozen golf balls. Translate that into terms of wagering a week's rent and you can appreciate the kind of mess that it is possible to get into by agreeing to a bet you do not fully understand.

The soundest rule in golf gambling is to play it safe and keep it simple. A modest flutter may well add spice to the match but the moment anyone starts mentioning side bets and presses the best advice is to announce your limit and stick to it. You can always console yourself with the noble thought that you are acting within the spirit of the rules of amateur status.

R.&A. POLICY ON GAMBLING

"Amateur golf is a game to be played for its own sake and not for profit. When gambling motives are introduced evils can arise to threaten the integrity of both the game and the individual players. The R. & A. therefore urges Unions and Clubs to dissociate themselves from all forms of organised gambling, particularly auction sweepstakes connected with Open Handicap events or Pro./Ams. Attention is drawn to Rule 1-13 relating to conduct detrimental to the game, under which players can forfeit their amateur status. It is the Club which, by permitting competitions where excessive gambling is involved, or illegal prizes are offered, bears the responsibility for which the individual is penalised."

10 DECISIONS AND DISPUTES

A selection of notable decisions handed down by the Rules of Golf committees of the Royal and Ancient golf club of St Andrews and the United States Golf Association

The decisions which are handed down by the Rules of Golf committees are issued to interested bodies to clarify knotty points of golf law. Anyone can settle a dispute by appeal to the committees although it must be forwarded through a club or competition secretary. Individual queries cannot be accepted because that would need a large, full-time tribunal to handle the flood of requests to 'settle a bet'. In the vast majority of cases competition committees have enough expertise to resolve disputes and ambiguities and it is normally only when they are unsure of their ground that they put a case forward for arbitration – to the United States Golf Association from the American continent or to the Royal and Ancient Golf Club of St Andrews from the sixty nations affiliated to that body. By the time the decisions have been handed down and prepared for public distribution, they have been dehumanised to the level of those schoolbook mathematical problems involving *A* and *B* which members of the older generation will remember so well. Now, however, *A* and *B* are not competing with each other to fill a trench with water or to race each other on horseback or bicycle. They are trying their damnedest to win a golf match and the student who delves into the published volumes of decisions soon gets the feeling that it is the same *A* and *B* in every dispute. And, being golf, their wives are also heavily involved and continually at odds with each other.

The more one reads, the stronger this fantasy grows. The *A*s and *B*s emerge as distinct characters and with the unfolding of successive golfing contretemps their personalities are revealed. Mr and Mrs *A* are clearly the most unpopular people in the club. They are always ready for an argument and carry well-thumbed copies of the Rules of Golf wherever they go. Mr *A*, a thin, retired money-lender's clerk, is that tedious creature who compensates for his deficiencies by insisting on his rights on every possible occasion. 'We'll soon settle this,' he is fond of announcing, 'we'll get the secretary to write to the Rules of Golf Committee.' He does not have an inferiority complex, he *is* inferior and so is his golf. Years of signing orders to repossess television sets and motor cars has drained all the humanity from his breast. His thin-lipped wife, a wiry shrew, with a voice which can shatter a wine glass at normal conversational pitch, is the perfect soul-mate for him. They are childless and embittered and spend their evenings writing poison-pen letters to the chairman of the Rules of Golf Committee in response to adverse judgements. For them golf is not so much a game as a war, total war.

How, you may ask, do such a cantankerous pair come to play so much golf with the popular Bs? Well, the Bs are over-endowed with human kindness. They overflow with brotherly love and if you really want the truth of it, they befriend the As out of pity. 'Why those poor folk would never get a game if it wasn't for us,' Mr B once confided to his wife. 'I've always said that there is good in everyone and I mean to discover some of it in those two.' Mr B, who laughs readily and heartily, used to own a grocery shop and was famous for the way he would slip a bar of chocolate into the order of a family when he knew the father was down on his luck. His good nature spills out into his golf. He is absurdly generous in the matter of conceding putts, partly through natural kindness and partly because he enjoys a keen finish. He is slightly a better player than A and this is one way of keeping them on level terms. He nearly always loses and pays up with good grace.

Mrs B is a cheerful soul with an ample figure which bears witness to the excellence of her cooking. She is inclined to be vague and her reputation for coolness in a crisis springs more from her failure to recognise the seriousness of events than to innate phlegm. When cataclysmic world news is announced, she responds with her favourite phrase, 'I am sure the government will do what's best for us' and quietly goes about her chores. She takes in stray cats and dogs and regards the As in much the same light, as underprivileged creatures in need of help and comfort. She has only a passing acquaintance with the rules and most of the time she accepts the penalties which are called on her by Mrs A with cheerful stoicism. After all, they play for only a penny a hole. The strength of her game rests in her disregard for conventional golfing styles. Not for her the statuesque finish with hands held high nor a slavish regard for golfing fashions. She knocks the ball along with whatever club she feels at the time to be appropriate, and when she gets a bad lie alongside the out-of-bounds wall, she frequently extricates her ball by bashing at it left-handed with the back of her putter. This club has a heavy flange which serves to turn it into a lofted club when wielded backwards.

Having been soundly beaten on one occasion by Mrs *B*'s ambidexterity, Mrs *A* sat in the ladies locker room furiously studying Appendix II of the Rules of Golf which, as everyone knows, concerns the shape and form of the facings of golf clubs. Mrs *A* quickly concluded that, regardless of the legality of Mrs *B*'s putter when used right-handed, it certainly did not conform to the legal specifications as a left-handed club. She insisted that the competitions secretary write to the Rules of Golf Committee for a decision. 'It is not the money but the principle of the affair,' she insisted. Alas for Mrs *A*, the committee (Decision 58/93/64) ruled that there was no objection to hitting the ball with the back of a club.

Mr and Mrs *A* rely heavily on Rule 11 in their litigious battles because this is the rule involving disputes. As soon as a point of doubt arises the barrack-room lawyer with a thorough knowledge of Rule 11 has an enormous advantage. By following the correct procedure, he can win the day even though all the principles of natural justice and equity are against him. A good example of how legal training can prevail over skill occurred in a match between Mr *A* and Mr *B*. For once Mr *A* hit the longer tee shot but since it was down the wide side of a dog-legged fairway, Mr *B*'s tee-shot actually finished nearer the hole. 'It is your shot,' he called, as they walked up to their balls. 'Oh no,' said the devious Mr *A*, 'it is you to play first because the rules say that the player nearest the tee plays first.'

By now, we all know that to be rubbish and we may suspect that Mr *A*, the rules king, was deliberately trying to pull a fast one. But bumbling Mr *B*, unsure of his facts and not wanting to make an issue of it, went ahead and played. The exchange had unsettled him because he believed that regardless of the Rules of Golf there must be some special local rule, known to Mr *A*, which governed this particular case. Anyway, with his mind in a turmoil he hit his shot and lost the hole. And the match. Afterwards Mr *B* was talking about the incident in the club-house and his friends indignantly insisted that he should have won the hole, on the grounds that the odious Mr *A* had given him wrong information. The Rules of Golf Committee considered the incident and found in favour of Mr *A*. 'It is the duty of all players to be conversant with the rules and local rules', the committee pontificated with a pomposity and disregard for justice which makes the imagination boggle. Even if we accept that Mr *A* acted innocently when he insisted that Mr *B* play first, contrary to the rules, he was in the wrong and should have been the one to suffer. That case should serve as a warning to us all not only to learn the rules but to be wary of information given by other golfers. If there is any doubt in match-play, you should make a claim before the hole is completed. Preferably the dispute should be settled before the next hole is played but in practice it is not always possible to get hold of a referee or a committee ruling. In that case, provided the player in dispute has formally announced his disagreement to his opponent, the hole should be played out, leaving the result in abeyance until the players can get an official ruling. The result of the match can then be adjusted, if necessary, but this is an undesirable practice and should be used only in the last resort. It is highly unsatisfactory and unsettling to continue a match not knowing whether you are one up, all square or possibly one down. All the more reason to learn the rules and carry a copy of them in your golf bag so that you can clear up contentious points there and then to the mutual satisfaction of both players.

In stroke-play you have the option in disputed cases to play an alternative ball but then, remember, you must accept the score with the alternative ball if the committee later rules it to be legal.

Now for another little tangle between Mr *A* and Mr *B*. They were playing a match and at the 16th hole, Mr *A* hit his second shot out of bounds. He dropped another ball, played on to the green and two-putted. (Add it up. Drive, second shot out of bounds, penalty stroke, approach shot, two putts = 6.) Mr *B* took three shots to reach the green and also two-putted. As they walked off the green Mr *B* said 'A half?' and Mr *A* said 'Yes'. Mr *A* won the match and that evening Mr *B*, sleeplessly reflecting on the round, realised that Mr *A* had actually taken six strokes to his five on the 16th. For once his benign nature was roused to lodge a claim to the competition committee. The claim was passed on to the Rules of Golf Committee who blandly replied that Mr *B* presumably knew about Mr *A*'s penalty stroke (Rule 10 insists that a player who has incurred a penalty stroke must inform his opponent or marker as soon as possible). Mr *B* was not claiming to have been misled by Mr *A*, the misunderstanding was mutual. Therefore the result must stand as a half and the result of the match as a win for Mr *A*.

The same Rule 10 also entitles a player to ask his opponent at any time in a match how many strokes he has taken. If your opponent gives you wrong information – and fails to correct it before you play your next shot – then he loses the hole. A good lawyer might have submitted to the appeal court that when Mr *B* said 'A half?' he was in effect enquiring whether Mr *A* had also taken five strokes. In that event Mr *A*'s reply of 'Yes' would have constituted wrong information under Rule 10 and loss of hole. We shall never know whether the Rules of Golf Committee would have accepted that argument. Probably not. Provided that there is no collusion to ignore a rule of golf (which means disqualification of all concerned under Rule 4) there is nothing to stop players agreeing to a half.

Mr *A* had another triumph against the hapless Mr *B* when they both landed in the same bunker with their balls lying close together. Mr *A* had to play first and in the process of firmly grounding his feet in the sand he raised a mound of sand behind Mr *B*'s ball, giving him an immeasurably more difficult shot when it came his turn to play. 'I hope you are going to smooth out that mountain you have made behind my ball', said Mr *B*. 'I am sorry, friend,' replied Mr *A*, 'but I cannot do that. In doing so I might move your ball and that would cost me a penalty. It is bad luck on you but there is nothing I can do about it.' The Rules of Golf Committee confirmed that Mr *A* was not obliged to smooth his footprints. What Mr *B* should have done, if only he had known his rights, was to have lifted his ball and dropped it as near as possible to the spot where it was without penalty, to give him a lie like his original one. There is a well-established principle in golf under the rule of equity (Rule 11–4) that a player is normally entitled to the lie which his stroke gave him. That means he is entitled to relief from the actions of opponents, fellow competitors and outside agencies. A similar situation would arise if you hit a drive down the middle of the fairway into a perfect lie and while you were walking forward a tractor passed by your stationary ball and it was toppled into a rut. The strictly legalistic decisions of the Rules of Golf Committee often appear harsh and manifestly unjust compared to the decisions of competition committees operating on the principles of common sense and natural justice. For once both Mr *A* and Mr *B* were genuinely mistaken about the result of a match. They were under the impression that Mr *A* had taken it by one hole and gave in that result to the competitions secretary. While they were changing their shoes in the locker room and talking over the game, they realised they had made a mistake and in fact had been all square after the 18th. They explained their predicament to the competition committee who ordered them to replay. That seemed the sensible thing to do but since no rule appeared to cover this contingency, a ruling was requested from the Rules of Golf Committee. That august body replied that the original recorded result of a win for Mr *A* should have stood.

One of the problems which the long-suffering Rules of Golf Committee has to solve is the application of the old rules and principles to new equipment. New clubs and balls have to conform to the official specification, but that does not necessarily mean that they will always conform to golfing orthodoxy. An example is the solid, or 'one-piece', golf ball which is really a direct descendant of the old guttie. The modern version made of polysyllabic plastic has many virtues, notably relative cheapness and durability. However, it is not always quite as totally indestructible as the makers would have us believe. It sometimes splits into pieces on impact from the club. What does the poor golfer do now, especially if one of the pieces has flown out of bounds?

Well, if your club breaks while you are making a shot that is doubly your bad luck, because you not only have to pay for a repair but you have to count the stroke as well. That, too, used to be more or less the procedure with a split ball. You counted that shot and substituted another ball (under the 'Ball unfit for play' rule) in the presence of your opponent or marker. If the larger lump had flown out of bounds, then that was tough luck. You had to follow the out-of-bounds procedures. After a year's operation of this harsh dictum, the Rules of Golf Committee had second and more humane thoughts. It is now decreed that if your ball shatters into pieces you do not count that stroke at all. You simply drop another ball on the same spot or tee up another if the fissure occurred on the tee. The committee solemnly adds that if a ball splits on the green then you may place another, although so far no golfer has appeared with a putting stroke so violent as to shatter an 'indestructible' ball. You never know, though, and it is comforting to know that the rule is ready and waiting for that unlikely contingency.

Finally, let us end this section on doubts and uncertainties by returning to those golfing Montagues and Capulets, Mr *A* and Mr *B*. Or rather let us leave the last word to their wives, for the expression about the female of the species being deadlier than the male applies to no specimens more strongly than to women golfers. The ladies were playing a match and Mrs *B* had the misfortune to hit her ball into a bunker beside the green. Her discomforture was somewhat increased to notice a rattlesnake basking in the warm sunshine near the ball. What should she do? Mrs *A* quickly consulted her rule book just to confirm her first impression and then said: 'I am sorry, dear, but there is nothing else for it; you have to play the ball as it lies. The rules say so.' Mrs *B* hesitated. 'It is quite clear', continued Mrs *A*, 'that you cannot touch or move a loose impediment like a snake in a hazard.' Mrs *B* responded to the effect that she was more concerned about the possibility, indeed probability, that the snake might touch her. 'Oh, don't be so silly,' said Mrs *A*, 'you are behaving like a frightened schoolgirl. I'll tell you what I'll do. Rule 9 on advice and assistance says that in making a stroke a player shall not seek or accept physical assistance or protection from the elements. So although it may be slightly contrary to the rule against giving protection, I am prepared to stand guard with a rake. Don't worry. If the brute starts to attack you I will give it a good whack.' 'You are too kind', said Mrs *B* with heavy sarcasm. 'There's no need to adopt that tone,' said Mrs *A*, 'after all, I'm taking a risk myself. Who knows, I might be liable to a penalty for playing out of turn, or using an illegal club. Knowing our competitions secretary, the bitch would certainly make me count it as an air shot at the very least.'

Mrs *B* was torn between the idea of forfeiting the hole; or of using her wedge on the rattlesnake, thereby risking a penalty for 'testing the surface'; or of hitting Mrs *A* over the head with a sand-iron and pushing her into the bunker alongside her natural counterpart. The Rules of Golf Committee immediately put its legal finger on the flaw in Mrs *A*'s reasoning. Worms and insects are loose impediments but not rattlesnakes. They are outside agencies, not that it made any material difference in this situation. Most legal problems can be solved by precedent and there have been numerous examples in the past of golfers being exonerated for putting their personal safety above the outcome of a match. Rule 37, for instance, permits a player to discontinue play without penalty, if he is stricken by a sudden illness 'which the committee considers satisfactory'. Most committees consider heart attacks satisfactory and positively purr with satisfaction over broken limbs. There were further precedents. In Africa special local rules have been approved to permit golfers to drop clear of dangerous wild animals. And in wartime Britain, players were allowed free drops from the vicinity of unexploded bombs. The Rules of Golf committees are not totally heartless about the physical safety of golfers and so the case of the snake in the bunker presented no great difficulty. The committee ruled that it was not reasonable to expect Mrs B to play from such a dangerous situation.

In this instance Mrs B could have acted under the rule of equity (11–4) and placed a ball in the hazard in a situation which she did not consider dangerous, as near as possible and in a similar lie. She might even in these special circumstances have placed a ball in a different and rattler-free hazard in which the conditions were otherwise much the same as the original bunker. So much for disputes. Perhaps it is appropriate to end with a word about referees who have been properly appointed by competition committees to arbitrate on questions of fact and law. If you have occasion to refer any point to a referee you must abide by his decision. Referees are fallible and they make mistakes. By all means put your case as skilfully as you can, quoting chapter and verse of the appropriate rules from your personal rule book.

But once the referee has made his decision you must accept. Right or wrong, his decision is final.

GLOSSARY

ADDRESS   A golfer has addressed his ball as soon as he has taken his stance and grounded his club behind the ball. In a hazard, where it is not permitted to ground the club, taking a stance constitutes the address. The importance of the definitions is that if a ball moves after a player has addressed it, he is judged to have caused the ball to move and must count a penalty stroke.

ADVICE   Any suggestion which could influence a golfer in making up his mind how to play, what club to use or the method of playing a stroke is advice. It can be sought or accepted only from a player's partner or either of their caddies. Information on rules or local rules is not advice, nor is information about the line of play for a hole.

ALBATROSS   A score of three below the par for a hole.

ATTENDING THE FLAG   A player is entitled to have the flag attended and held up to indicate the position of the hole at any time. On the green it is an infringement for a ball (played from on the green) to strike an unattended flagstick.

BACK MARKER   The low-handicap player in a match. It is customary to compute stroke allowances for matches by reducing the back marker's handicap to scratch.

BAFFIE   Type of obsolete wooden club approximating to the modern 4-wood.

BEST BALL   A match in which one player competes against the best ball of two or three other players.

BIRDIE   A score of one below the par for a hole.

BISQUE   A handicap stroke which a player can elect to take at any time during a match.

BLASTER   A broad-soled wedge.

BOGEY   Standard American terminology (and spreading) for a score of one more than the par for a hole. Thus double-bogey, triple-bogey etc. Derives from the obsolescent system of rating golf courses according to the number of strokes a scratch player would be expected to take, therefore on longer and more difficult holes a stroke higher than par.

BRASSIE   Old term for 2-wood.

BULGER   Driver with a pronouncedly convex face.

BUNKER   Hazard consisting of an area of bare earth, or sand, usually in the form of a depression. Grass banks and artificial walls of bunkers are not part of the hazard.

BYE   A secondary match played over the remaining holes after the main match has been completed.

CADDIE   A person employed to carry a player's clubs and offer advice. Players are responsible for the actions of their caddies and suffer penalties for any infringement of rule by their caddies.

CASUAL WATER   Any temporary accumulation of water which is clearly visible after the player has taken his stance. Snow and ice may be treated as casual water or loose impediments at the discretion of the player.

CHIP   A low, running shot played from just off the green.

COMPETITOR   Player in a stroke-play competition. A fellow competitor is a player he accompanies during play and may be his marker. A fellow competitor is not a partner within the rules.

CUT   General term to denote a shot, deliberate or accidental, which causes the ball to move from left to right through the air. It thus covers both fades and slices.

DEAD   A ball is said to be dead when it lies so close to the hole as to make the putt a formality.

DIVOT   A slice of turf displaced in making a shot. It is one of the canons of golf etiquette that divots should be replaced and firmly trodden into position.

DORMIE, DORMY   A player (or side) is said to be dormie when he is as many holes up in the match as there are holes left to be played and he therefore cannot be beaten. The expression is believed to derive from the French verb *dormir* since the player can go to sleep and still not be beaten.

DRAW   An intentional stroke which causes the ball to move in a controlled manner from right to left through the air.

EAGLE   A score of two under the par of a hole.

ECLECTIC   A total arrived at by taking the best scores at each hole from a number of stroke-play cards returned by the same player.

EQUIPMENT   Anything used, worn or carried by a player or his caddie, including golf carts and trolleys, but not his ball in play.

FADE   An intentional stroke which causes the ball to move from left to right through the air in a controlled manner.

FAIRWAY   The mown portion of the playing area of a course between the tee and green. The rules of golf do not distinguish between fairways and rough (although special local rules may). In the rules, all of a course except the teeing-ground and the green of the hole being played, and all hazards on the course, are defined as 'through the green'.

FAT   A golfer is said to have hit the ball 'fat' when his club-head contacts the ground before striking the ball. Also used to describe the heart of the green – for example: 'I ignored the flag and aimed for the fat of the green.'

FEATHERIE   Early type of golf ball traditionally made by stuffing a top-hatful of feathers into a hide casing.

FLAGSTICK   Movable indicator to mark the position of a hole. Colloquially referred to as pin, flag or stick.

FORE!   Conventional golfer's cry to warn players ahead of an approaching ball.

FORECADDIE   A person employed by a competition committee to mark the landing of golf balls, specially on blind holes and in areas of excessive rough.

FOUR-BALL   A match in which two players play their better ball against the better ball of two other partners.

FOURSOME   A form of partner golf in which players take alternate shots at the same ball. Commonly known as Scotch Foursomes in America.

GREEN   The prepared putting surface. A ball is on the green when any part of it touches the green.

GREENSOME   A modification of foursomes golf, with both partners driving at each hole and selecting the preferred ball with which to complete the hole in alternate strokes.

GROUND UNDER REPAIR   Any part of the course marked as such by the committee; material piled for removal.

GUTTIE   Obsolete type of ball made from gutta percha.

HALF   A hole completed in the same net scores by both sides in matchplay is said to result in a half, or to be halved. Also used in the same sense to describe the result of a drawn match.

HANGING LIE   A lie on sloping ground which forces the golfer to play from an uneven stance.

HAZARD   Any bunker or water hazard defined as such by the committee.

HOLE   The hole is standardised at 4¼ in. in diameter (108mm) and at least 4 in. (100mm) deep. If a liner is used it must be sunk at least 1 in. below the surface.

HOLED   A ball is judged to be holed when all of it lies within the circumference of the hole and below the lip.

HONOUR   The privilege of playing first from the tee.

HOOK   An unintentional stroke which causes the ball to fly from right to left through the air in an uncontrolled manner.

HOSEL   The neck of an iron club into which the shaft is fitted.

JIGGER   A specialist club for run-up shots.

LIKE   A player is said to be 'playing the like' when he is taking a shot which makes his score the same as his opponent's.

LINE OF PLAY   Usually abbreviated to 'the line', as in 'What is the line on this hole?' Means the preferred route.

LINKS   A golf course built on linksland by the sea. Sometimes used loosely as another term for a golf course of any kind.

LOCAL RULES   Rules formulated by local committees to cover special conditions on the course.

LOFT   The angle by which a club-face is set back from the perpendicular.

LOOSE IMPEDIMENTS   Natural objects, not fixed or growing. Includes stones if not firmly embedded, fallen twigs and leaves, dung, worms and insects, and casts made by them. Sand and loose soil are classified as loose impediments on the green but not through the green. Snow and ice may be classified as loose impediments or casual water, at the discretion of the player.

LOST BALL   A ball is declared to be lost if it is not found within five minutes; or if the owner puts another ball into play; or if the player formally abandons his ball, whether or not he searches for it; or if he plays any stroke with a provisional ball beyond the place where the original ball was likely to be.

MARKER   A person, often a fellow competitor, charged with keeping a competitor's score. It is, however, the responsibility of the player to ensure the accuracy of his score.

MASHIE   An old, lofted iron club roughly equivalent to a 5-iron.

MASHIE-NIBLICK   An old club, as above, approximating a 7-iron.

MATCH-PLAY   The form of golf which is contested on the number of holes won, rather than by the total number of strokes taken for a round (stroke-play). Special rules operate for match-play golf.

MEDAL-PLAY   Stroke-play.

MOVED BALL   A ball is judged to have moved if it comes to rest in another position. Rocking, or oscillation, does not count as movement for purposes of penalty at the address provided the ball settles back into its original position.

MULLIGAN   The practice, quite unofficial, of allowing a player a 'free' second drive when his first shot is unsatisfactory.

NAP   Sometimes called grain. It is the texture of a putting surface caused by grasses tending to lie in the same direction.

NASSAU   A form of wager involving a three-way bet: on the first nine holes, on the second nine, and a similar amount on the match as a whole.

NIBLICK   An old club roughly equal to a 9-iron.

OBSERVER   A person appointed by the committee to help a referee decide questions of fact and report any infringements.

OBSTRUCTION   Anything artificial erected, placed or left on the course, except boundary fences, walls and stakes and artificial roads and paths. The committee may decree any such to be an integral part of the course in which case the rules for relief from obstructions do not apply.

ODD   A player is said to be playing the odd when he is taking a shot which makes his score one more than his opponent's.

OUT OF BOUNDS   A ball is out of bounds when all of it lies over a line drawn between the nearest inside points of boundary stakes. If a line is used to define a boundary the line itself is out of bounds.

OUTSIDE AGENCY   Any agency not part of the match. In stroke-play outside agencies include referees, markers, fellow competitors and observers.

PAR   The norm for a hole. In most countries par is set exclusively on length. Holes up to 250 yards are par-3; 251–475 yards are par-4; 476 yards and over are par-5.

PARTNER   A player on the same side.

PENALTY   A stroke, or strokes, to be added to the score under the rules. Penalty strokes do not affect the order of play in foursomes or greensomes.

PIN HIGH   A shot finishing level with the flagstick is said to be pin high, therefore a perfect length but not necessarily straight.

PITCH   A high, floating shot. Normally used to describe such shots played to a green.

PRESS   The act of spoiling a shot by hitting too hard. Also, in wagering, a subsidiary bet which can be instituted over the remaining holes when a side becomes two down in the main match.

PULL   An unintentional shot which flies in a straight line to the left of the target.

PUSH   Opposite of pull. In this case the ball goes in a straight line right of target.

PUTT   A stroke played with a putter.

REFEREE   A person appointed by a committee to accompany players and rule on questions of fact and golf law. His decision is final.

ROUND ROBIN   A type of match-play competition in which every entrant plays against everyone else, the person with the most victories being the winner.

RUBBER CORE   A ball made by winding rubber thread under tension around a central core and then covering with a plastic casing. This is the universal method of manufacturing the highest grade balls.

RUB OF THE GREEN   The expression to cover the case of a moving ball being stopped or deflected by an outside agency. Commonly it is used to describe any piece of golfing luck, good or bad, for which there is no provision in the rules.

SAND WEDGE   Specialist club for playing recovery shot from sand.

SCRATCH   The handicap mark of a first-class player. Methods of computing scratch ratings vary from country to country but loosely the term can be said to cover golfers who can regularly play par golf off the competition tees in summer conditions. Scratch players get no handicap allowance, hence scratch competitions are those in which no handicap strokes are given.

SHANK (SOCKET)   A stroke in which the hosel, or neck, of the club makes contact with the ball, sending it off at an acute angle.

SLICE   Unintentional shot which causes the ball to veer from left to right in an uncontrolled manner through the air.

SPOON   Obsolescent term for 3-wood.

STABLEFORD   Form of golf in which players count one point for a score of one over the par of a hole, two points for par, three points for a birdie – and so on.

STANCE   The placing of the feet in position in preparation for making a stroke. A stance is not necessarily an address.

STROKE   A forward movement of the club made with the intention of fairly striking the ball.

STROKE-PLAY   Also known as medal-play. The system of golf in which a player counts his total of strokes for a round.

TEE   A peg for teeing the ball or the prepared area on which the teeing-ground is sited.

TEEING-GROUND   A rectangle two club-lengths in depth measured back from a line between the markers.

TEXAS WEDGE   American term for a shot played from off the green with a putter.

THREE-BALL   A match in which three players each play against the two others.

THREESOME   A match in which one player plays against two partners playing alternate shots at one ball.

THROUGH THE GREEN   The whole area of the course except all hazards and the teeing-ground and the green of the hole being played.

TOP   The action of striking the ball's top half, producing a low, scuttling shot.

TRAP   Colloquialism for bunker.

WAGGLE   Preliminary movement of the club at address before making a stroke.

WEDGE   Broad-soled club designed for pitching.

WINTER RULES   Special local rules employed by committees to protect the course in winter. Conventions vary from club to club and players should always check the local rules to determine the type and degree of relief which is permissible.

The Rules of Golf

Section I Etiquette

Courtesy on the Course

Consideration for Other Players
In the interest of all, players should play without delay.
No player should play until the players in front are out of range.
Players searching for a ball should signal the players behind them to pass as soon as it becomes apparent that the ball will not easily be found; they should not search for five minutes before doing so. They should not continue play until the players following them have passed and are out of range.
When the play of a hole has been completed, players should immediately leave the putting green.

Behaviour During Play
No one should move, talk or stand close to or directly behind the ball or the hole when a player is addressing the ball or making a stroke.
The player who has the honour should be allowed to play before his opponent or fellow-competitor tees his ball.

Priority on the Course

In the absence of special rules, two-ball matches should have precedence of and be entitled to pass any three- or four-ball match.
A single player has no standing and should give way to a match of any kind.
Any match playing a whole round is entitled to pass a match playing a shorter round.
If a match fails to keep its place on the course and loses more than one clear hole on the players in front, it should allow the match following to pass.

Care of the Course

Holes in Bunkers
Before leaving a bunker, a player should carefully fill up and smooth over all holes and footprints made by him.

Restore Divots, Repair Ball-Marks and Damage by Spikes
Through the green, a player should ensure that any turf cut or displaced by him is replaced at once and pressed down, and that any damage to the putting green made by the ball is carefully repaired. Damage to the putting green caused by golf shoe spikes should be repaired *on completion of the hole.*

Damage to Greens—Flagsticks, Bags, etc.
Players should ensure that, when putting down bags, or the flagstick, no damage is done to the putting green, and that neither they nor their caddies damage the hole by standing close to it, in handling the flagstick or in removing the ball from the hole. The flagstick should be properly replaced in the hole before the players leave the putting green.

Golf Carts
Local Notices regulating the movement of golf carts should be strictly observed.

Damage through Practice Swings
In taking practice swings, players should avoid causing damage to the course, particularly the tees, by removing divots.

Section II Definitions

1. Addressing the Ball
A player has "addressed the ball" when he has taken his stance and has also grounded his club, except that in a hazard a player has addressed the ball when he has taken his stance.

2. Advice
"Advice" is any counsel or suggestion which could influence a player in determining his play, the choice of a club, or the method of making a stroke.
Information on the Rules or Local Rules is not advice.

3. Ball Deemed to Move
A ball is deemed to have "moved" if it leave its position and come to rest in any other place.

4. Ball Holed
A ball is "holed" when it lies within the circumference of the hole and all of it is below the level of the lip of the hole.

5. Ball in Play, Provisional Ball, Wrong Ball
a. A ball is "in play" as soon as the player has made a stroke on the teeing ground. It remains as his ball in play until holed out, except when it is out of bounds, lost or lifted, or another ball has been substituted under an applicable Rule or Local Rule: a ball so substituted becomes the ball in play.
b. A provisional ball" is a ball played under Rule 30 for a ball which may be lost outside a water hazard or may be out of bounds. It ceases to be a provisional ball when the Rule provides *either* that the player continue play with it as the ball in play *or* that it be abandoned.
c. A "wrong ball" is any ball other than the ball in play or a provisional ball or, in stroke play, an alternate ball played in accordance with Rule 11-5.

6. Ball Lost
A ball is "lost" if:—
a. It be not found, or be not identified as his by the player, within five minutes after the player's side or his or their caddies have begun to search for it; *or*

b. The player has put another ball into play under the Rules, even though he may not have searched for the original ball; *or*

c. The player has played any stroke with a provisional ball from a point beyond the place where the original ball is likely to be, whereupon the provisional ball becomes the ball in play.

Time spent in playing a wrong ball is not counted in the five-minute period allowed for search.

7. Caddie, Forecaddie and Equipment

a. A "caddie" is one who carries or handles a player's clubs during play and otherwise assists him in accordance with the Rules.

When one caddie is employed by more than one player, he is always deemed to be the caddie of the player whose ball is involved, and equipment carried by him is deemed to be that player's equipment, except when the caddie acts upon specific directions of another player, in which case he is considered to be that other player's caddie.

Note: *In threesome, foursome, best-ball and four-ball play, a caddie carrying for more than one player should be assigned to the members of one side.*

b. A "forecaddie" is one employed by the Committee to indicate to players the position of balls on the course, and is an outside agency (Definition 22).

c. "Equipment" is anything used, worn or carried by or for the player except his ball in play. Equipment includes a golf cart. If such a cart is shared by more than one player, its status under the Rules is the same as that of a caddie employed by more than one player.

8. Casual Water

"Casual water" is any temporary accumulation of water which is visible before or after the player takes his stance and which is not a hazard of itself or is not in a water hazard. Snow and ice are either casual water or loose impediments, at the option of the player.

9. Committee

The "Committee" is the committee in charge of the competition.

10. Competitor

A "competitor" is a player in a stroke competition. A "fellow-competitor" is any person with whom the competitor plays. Neither is partner of the other.

In stroke play foursome and four-ball competitions, where the context so admits, the word "competitor" or "fellow-competitor" shall be held to include his partner.

11. Course

The "course" is the whole area within which play is permitted. It is the duty of the Committee to define its boundaries accurately.

12. Flagstick

The "flagstick" is a movable straight indicator provided by the Committee, with or without bunting or other material attached, centred in the hole to show its position. It shall be circular in cross-section.

13. Ground Under Repair

"Ground under repair" is any portion of the course so marked by order of the committee concerned or so declared by its authorised representative. It includes material piled for removal and a hole made by a greenkeeper, even if not so marked. Stakes and lines defining ground under repair are not in such ground.

14. Hazards
A "hazard" is any bunker or water hazard. Bare patches, scrapes, roads, tracks and paths are not hazards.

a. A "bunker" is an area of bare ground, often a depression, which is usually covered with sand. Grass-covered ground bordering or within a bunker is *not* part of the hazard.

b. A "water hazard" is any sea, lake, pond, river, ditch, surface drainage ditch or other open water course (regardless of whether or not it contains water), and anything of a similar nature.
All ground or water within the margin of a water hazard, whether or not it be covered with any growing substance, is part of the water hazard. The margin of a water hazard is deemed to extend vertically upwards.

c. A "lateral water hazard" is a water hazard or that part of a water hazard so situated that it is not possible or is deemed by the Committee to be impracticable to drop a ball behind the water hazard and keep the spot at which the ball last crossed the margin of the hazard between the player and the hole.

d. It is the duty of the Committee in charge of a course to define accurately the extent of the hazards and water hazards when there is any doubt. That part of a hazard to be played as a lateral water hazard should be distinctively marked. Stakes and lines defining the margins of hazards are not in the hazards.

15. Hole
The "hole" shall be $4\frac{1}{4}$ inches (108 mm) in diameter and at least 4 inches (100 mm) deep. If a lining be used, it shall be sunk at least 1 inch (25 mm) below the putting green surface unless the nature of the soil makes it impractical to do so; its outer diameter shall not exceed $4\frac{1}{4}$ inches (108 mm).

16. Honour
The side which is entitled to play first from the teeing ground is said to have the "honour."

17. Loose Impediments
The term "loose impediments" denotes natural objects not fixed or growing and not adhering to the ball, and includes stones not solidly embedded, leaves, twigs, branches and the like, dung, worms and insects and casts or heaps made by them.
Snow and ice are either casual water or loose impediments, at the option of the player.
Sand and loose soil are loose impediments on the putting green, but not elsewhere on the course.

18. Marker
A "marker" is a scorer in stroke play who is appointed by the Committee to record a competitor's score. He may be a fellow-competitor. He is not a referee.
A marker should not lift a ball or mark its position unless authorised to do so by the competitor and, unless he is a fellow-competitor, should not attend the flagstick or stand at the hole or mark its position.

19. Observer
An "observer" is appointed by the Committee to assist a referee to

decide questions of fact and to report to him any breach of a Rule or Local Rule. An observer should not attend the flagstick, stand at or mark the position of the hole, or lift the ball or mark its position.

20. Obstructions
An "obstruction" is anything artificial, whether erected, placed or left on the course, including the artificial surfaces and sides of roads and paths but excepting:–

a. Objects defining out of bounds, such as walls, fences, stakes and railings;

b. In water hazards, artificially surfaced banks or beds, including bridge supports when part of such a bank. Bridges and bridge supports which are not part of such a bank are obstructions;

c. Any construction declared by the Committee to be an integral part of the course.

21. Out of Bounds
"Out of bounds" is ground on which play is prohibited.

When out of bounds is fixed by stakes or a fence, the out of bounds line is determined by the nearest inside points of the stakes or fence posts at ground level; the line is deemed to extend vertically upwards. When out of bounds is fixed by a line on the ground, the line itself is out of bounds.

A ball is out of bounds when all of it lies out of bounds.

22. Outside Agency
An "outside agency" is any agency not part of the match or, in stroke play, not part of a competitor's side, and includes a referee, a marker, an observer, or a forecaddie employed by the Committee. Neither wind nor water is an outside agency.

23. Partner
A "partner" is a player associated with another player on the same side.

In a threesome, foursome or a four-ball, where the context so admits, the word "player" shall be held to include his partner.

24. Penalty Stroke
A "penalty stroke" is one added to the score of a side under certain Rules. It does not affect the order of play.

25. Putting Green
The "putting green" is all ground of the hole being played which is specially prepared for putting or otherwise defined as such by the Committee.

A ball is deemed to be on the putting green when any part of it touches the putting green.

26. Referee
A "referee" is a person who has been appointed by the Committee to accompany players to decide questions of fact and of golf law. He shall act on any breach of Rule or Local Rule which he may observe or which may be reported to him by an observer (Definition 19).

In stroke play the Committee may limit a referee's duties.

A referee should not attend the flagstick, stand at or mark the position of the hole, or lift the ball or mark its position.

27. Rub of the Green
A "rub of the green" occurs when a ball in motion is stopped or deflected by any outside agency.

28. Sides and Matches

Side: A player, or two or more players who are partners.

Single: A match in which one plays against another.

Threesome: A match in which one plays against two, and each side plays one ball.

Foursome: A match in which two play against two, and each side plays one ball.

Three-Ball: A match in which three play against one another, each playing his own ball.

Best-Ball: A match in which one plays against the better ball of two or the best ball of three players.

Four-Ball: A match in which two play their better ball against the better ball of two other players.

Note: *In a best-ball or four-ball match, if a partner be absent for reasons satisfactory to the Committee, the remaining member(s) of his side may represent the side.*

29. Stance

Taking the "stance" consists in a player placing his feet in position for and preparatory to making a stroke.

30. Stipulated Round

The "stipulated round" consists of playing the holes of the course in their correct sequence unless otherwise authorised by the Committee. The number of holes in a stipulated round is 18 unless a smaller number is authorised by the Committee.

In match play only, the Committee may, for the purpose of settling a tie, extend the stipulated round to as many holes as are required for a match to be won.

31. Stroke

A "stroke" is the forward movement of the club made with the intention of fairly striking at and moving the ball.

32. Teeing

In "teeing," the ball may be placed on the ground or on sand or other substance in order to raise it off the ground.

33. Teeing Ground

The "teeing ground" is the starting place for the hole to be played. It is a rectangular area two club-lengths in depth, the front and the sides of which are defined by the outside limits of two tee-markers. A ball is outside the teeing ground when all of it lies outside the stipulated area.

When playing the first stroke with any ball (including a provisional ball) from the teeing ground, the tee-markers are immovable obstructions (Definition 20).

34. Terms Used in Reckoning in Match Play

In match play, the reckoning of holes is kept by the terms:—so many "holes up" or "all square," and so many "to play."

A side is "dormie" when it is as many holes up as there are holes remaining to be played.

35. Through the Green

"Through the green" is the whole area of the course except:—

a. Teeing ground and putting green of the hole being played;

b. All hazards on the course.

36. Types of Club
There are three recognised types of golf club:—
An "iron" club is one with a head which usually is relatively narrow from face to back, and usually is made of steel.
A "wood" club is one with a head relatively broad from face to back, and usually is made of wood, plastic or a light metal.
A "putter" is a club designed primarily for use on the putting green—see Definition 25.

Section III The Rules of Play

Rule 1 The Game

The Game of Golf consists in playing a ball from the teeing ground into the hole by successive strokes in accordance with the Rules.
PENALTY FOR BREACH OF RULE:
Match play—Loss of hole; Stroke play—Disqualification.

Rule 2 The Club (*Def. 36*) and the Ball

The Royal and Ancient Golf Club and the United States Golf Association reserve the right to change the Rules and the interpretations regulating clubs and balls at any time.

1. Legal Clubs and Balls
The player's clubs, and the balls he uses, shall conform with Clauses 2 and 3 of this Rule.

2. Form and Make of Clubs
a. General Characteristics
The golf club shall be composed of a shaft and a head, and all of the various parts shall be fixed so that the club is one unit; the club shall not be designed to be adjustable, except for weight.
Note: *Playing characteristics not to be changed during a round—Rule 2-2b.*
The club shall not be substantially different from the traditional and customary form and make, and shall conform with the regulations governing the design of clubs at Appendix II and the specifications for markings on clubs at Appendix III.
b. Playing Characteristics Not to be Changed
The playing characteristics of a club shall not be purposely changed during a round; foreign material shall not be added to the club face at any time.
Note: *Players in doubt as to the legality of clubs are advised to consult the Royal and Ancient Golf Club of St. Andrews. If a manufacturer is in doubt as to the legality of a club which he proposes to manufacture, he should submit a sample to the Royal and Ancient Golf Club for a ruling, such sample to become the property of the Club for reference purposes.*

3. The Ball

a. Specifications

The weight of the ball shall be *not greater* than 1.620 ounces avoirdupois (45.93 gm) and the size *not less* than 1.620 inches (41.15 mm) in diameter.
The velocity of the ball shall be *not greater* than 250 feet (76.2 m) per second when measured on apparatus approved by the Royal and Ancient Golf Club of St. Andrews: a maximum tolerance of 2% will be allowed. The temperature of the ball when so tested shall be 75 degrees Fahrenheit (24 degrees Centigrade).
Note 1: *Under the Rules of the United States Golf Association the size of the ball shall be not less than 1.680 inches (42.67 mm) in diameter, but in international team competitions the size of the ball shall be not less than 1.620 inches (41.15 mm) in diameter.*
Note 2: *In laying down the conditions under which a competition is to be played (Rule 36-1) the Committee may stipulate that the ball to be used shall be of certain specifications provided these specifications are within the limits prescribed by Rule 2-3a.*

b. Foreign Material Prohibited

Foreign material shall not be applied to a ball for the purpose of changing its playing characteristics.
PENALTY FOR BREACH OF RULE: *Disqualification.*

Rule 3   Maximum of Fourteen Clubs

1. Selection and Replacement of Clubs

The player shall start a stipulated round with not more than fourteen clubs. He is limited to the clubs thus selected for that round except that, without unduly delaying play, he may:—
a. If he started with fewer than fourteen, add as many as will bring his total to that number;
b. Replace, with any club, a club which becomes unfit for play in the normal course of play.
The addition or replacement of a club or clubs may not be made by borrowing from any other person playing on the course.

2. Side May Share Clubs

Partners may share clubs provided that the total number of clubs carried by the side does not exceed fourteen.
PENALTY FOR BREACH OF RULE 3-1 OR 3-2, REGARDLESS OF NUMBER OF WRONG CLUBS CARRIED:
Match play—Loss of one hole for each hole at which any violation occurred; maximum penalty per round: loss of two holes. The penalty shall be applied to the state of the match at the conclusion of the hole at which the violation is discovered, provided all players in the match have not left the putting green of the last hole of the match.
Stroke play—Two strokes for each hole at which any violation occurred; maximum penalty per round: four strokes.

Stableford Competitions—From total points scored for the round, deduction of two points for each hole at which any violation occurred; maximum deduction per round: four points.
Note: *A serious breach of this Rule should be dealt with by the Committee under Rule 1.*

3. Wrong Club Declared Out of Play
Any club carried or used in violation of this Rule shall be declared out of play by the player immediately upon discovery and thereafter shall not be used by the player during the round *under penalty of disqualification.*

Rule 4   Agreement to Waive Rules Prohibited

Players shall not agree to exclude the operation of any Rule or Local Rule or to waive any penalty incurred.
PENALTY FOR BREACH OF RULE:
Match play—Disqualification of both sides; Stroke play—Disqualification of competitors concerned.

Rule 5   General Penalty

Except when otherwise provided for, the penalty for a breach of a Rule or Local Rule is:
Match play—Loss of hole; Stroke play—Two strokes.

Rule 6   Match Play

1. Winner of Hole
In match play the game is played by holes.
Except as otherwise provided for in the Rules, a hole is won by the side which holes its ball in the fewer strokes. In a handicap match the lower net score wins the hole.

2. Halved Hole
A hole is halved if each side holes out in the same number of strokes.
When a player has holed out and his opponent has been left with a stroke for the half, nothing that the player who has holed out can do shall deprive him of the half which he has already gained; but if the player thereafter incur any penalty, the hole is halved.

3. Winner of Match
A match (which consists of a stipulated round, unless otherwise decreed by the Committee) is won by the side which is leading by a number of holes greater than the number of holes remaining to be played.

Rule 7   Stroke Play

1. General Rule
The Rules for match play, so far as they are not at variance with specific Rules for stroke play, shall apply to stroke competitions. The converse is not true.

2. Winner
The competitor who holes the stipulated round or rounds in the fewest strokes is the winner.

3. Failure to Hole Out
If a competitor fail to hole out at any hole before he has played a stroke from the next teeing ground, or, in the case of the last hole of the round, before he has left the putting green, *he shall be disqualified.*
(*Ball purposely moved, touched or lifted—Rule 27-1c.*)

Rule 8   Practice

1. During Play of Hole
During the play of a hole, a player shall not play any practice stroke.
PENALTY FOR BREACH OF RULE 8-1:
Match play—Loss of hole; Stroke play—Two strokes.

2. Between Holes
Between the play of two holes, a player shall not play a practice stroke from any hazard, or on or to a putting green other than that of the hole last played.
PENALTY FOR BREACH OF RULE 8-2:
**Match play—Loss of hole; Stroke play—Two strokes.*
*The penalty applies to the next hole.

3. Stroke Play
On any day of a stroke competition or play-off, a competitor shall not practise on the competition course before a round or play-off. When a competition extends over consecutive days, practice on the competition course between rounds is prohibited.
If a competition extending over consecutive days is to be played on more than one course, practice between rounds on any competition course remaining to be played is prohibited.
Note: *The Committee may, at its discretion, waive or modify these prohibitions in the conditions of the competition (Appendix I-3).*
PENALTY FOR BREACH OF RULE 8-3: *Disqualification.*
(*Duty of Committee to define practice ground—Rule 36-4b.*)

Note 1: *A practice swing is not a practice stroke and may be taken at any place on the course provided the player does not violate the Rules.*
Note 2: *Unless otherwise decided by the Committee, there is no penalty for practice on the course on any day of a match play competition.*

Rule 9   Advice (*Def. 2*) and Assistance

1. Giving or Asking for Advice; Receiving Assistance
a. Advice
A player may give advice to, or ask for advice from, only his partner or either of their caddies..
b. Assistance
In making a stroke, a player shall not seek or accept physical assistance or protection from the elements.

2. Indicating Line of Play
Except on the putting green, a player may have the line of play indicated to him by anyone, but no mark shall be placed to indicate the line, nor shall anyone stand on or close to the line while the stroke is being played.
(*Indicating line of play on putting green—Rule 35-1e.*)
PENALTY FOR BREACH OF RULE:
Match play—Loss of hole; Stroke play—Two strokes.

Rule 10   Information as to Strokes Taken

1. General
A player who has incurred a penalty shall state the fact to his opponent or marker as soon as possible. The number of strokes a player has taken shall include any penalty strokes incurred.

2. Match Play
A player is entitled at any time during the play of a hole to ascertain from his opponent the number of strokes the latter has taken. If the opponent give wrong information as to the number of strokes he has taken and correct his mistake before the player has played his next stroke, he shall incur no penalty; if he fail to do so, *he shall lose the hole.*

Rule 11   Disputes, Decisions and Doubt as to Rights

1. Claims and Penalties
a. Match Play
In match play, if a dispute or doubt arise between the players on any

point, in order that a claim may be considered it must be made before any player in the match plays from the next teeing ground, or, in the case of the last hole of the match, before all players in the match leave the putting green. Any later claim based on newly discovered facts cannot be considered unless the player making the claim had been given wrong information by an opponent.

b. Stroke Play
In stroke play no penalty shall be imposed after the competition is closed unless wrong information had been given by the competitor. A competition is deemed to have closed:—
In stroke play only—When the result of the competition is officially announced;
In stroke play qualifying followed by match play—When the player has teed off in his first match.

2. Referee's Decision
If a referee has been appointed by the Committee, his decision shall be final.

3. Committee's Decision
In the absence of a referee, the players shall refer any dispute to the Committee, whose decision shall be final.
If the Committee cannot come to a decision, it shall refer the dispute to the Rules of Golf Committee of the Royal and Ancient Golf Club of St. Andrews, whose decision shall be final.
If the point in dispute or doubt has not been referred to the Rules of Golf Committee, the player or players have the right to refer an agreed statement through the Secretary of the Club to the Rules of Golf Committee for an opinion as to the correctness of the decision given. The reply will be sent to the Secretary of the Club or Clubs concerned.
If play be conducted other than in accordance with the Rules of Golf, the Rules of Golf Committee will not give a decision on any question.

4. Decision by Equity
If any point in dispute be not covered by the Rules or Local Rules, the decision shall be made in accordance with equity.

5. Stroke Play: Doubt as to Procedure
In stroke play only, when a competitor is doubtful of his rights or procedure, he may play out the hole with both the original ball and, at the same time, an alternate ball in a manner that he believes may be proper under the Rules for the given situation. The competitor's decision to invoke this Rule must be announced to his marker before the alternate ball is put into play and before any stroke is played with the original ball from the doubtful situation.
The competitor must complete the hole with both balls and, on completing the round, report the facts immediately to the Committee. If the Committee determine that the alternate ball was put into play in

accordance with the Rules, the score with the alternate ball shall count.

Note 1: *If the original ball is not immediately recoverable, the first ball put into play shall be treated as the original ball.*

Note 2: *The sole purpose of this Rule is to enable a competitor to avoid disqualification when doubtful of his rights or procedure.*

Note 3: *The privilege of playing an alternate ball does not exist in match play. An alternate ball played under Rule 11-5 is not a provisional ball under Rule 30.*

PENALTY FOR BREACH OF RULE 11-5: *Two strokes.*

Note: *A serious breach of Rule 11-5 should be dealt with by the Committee under Rule 1.*

Rule 12   The Honour (*Def. 16*)

1. The Honour
a. Match Play
A match begins by each side playing a ball from the first teeing ground in the order of the draw. In the absence of a draw, the option of taking the honour shall be decided by lot.

The side which wins a hole shall take the honour at the next teeing ground. If a hole has been halved, the side which had the honour at the previous teeing ground shall retain it.

b. Stroke Play
The honour shall be taken as in match play.

2. Playing out of Turn
a. Match Play
If, on the teeing ground, a player play when his opponent should have played, the opponent may immediately require the player to abandon the ball so played and to play a ball in correct order, without penalty.

b. Stroke Play
If, on the teeing ground, a competitor by mistake play out of turn, no penalty shall be incurred and the ball shall be in play.

c. Second Ball from Tee
If a player play a second ball, including a provisional ball, from the tee, he should do so after the opponent or the fellow-competitor has played his first stroke. If a player play a second ball out of turn, the provisions of Clauses 2a and 2b of this Rule apply.

Rule 13   Playing Outside Teeing Ground (*Def. 33*)

1. Match Play
If a player, when starting a hole, play a ball from outside the teeing ground, the opponent may immediately require the player to replay the stroke, in which case the player shall tee a ball and play the stroke from within the teeing ground, without penalty.

2. Stroke Play

If a competitor, when starting a hole, play his first stroke from outside the teeing ground, he shall count that stroke and any subsequent stroke so played and then shall tee a ball and play from within the teeing ground, without penalty. If the competitor fail to rectify his mistake before making a stroke on the next teeing ground, or, in the case of the last hole of the round, before leaving the putting green, *he shall be disqualified.*

PENALTY FOR BREACH OF RULE 13-2: *Disqualification.*

Note: Stance. *A player may take his stance outside the teeing ground to play a ball within it.*

Rule 14 Ball Falling off Tee

If a ball, when not in play, fall off a tee or be knocked off a tee by the player in addressing it, it may be re-teed without penalty, but if a stroke be made at the ball in these circumstances, whether the ball be moving or not, the stroke shall be counted but no penalty shall be incurred.

Rule 15 Order of Play in Threesome or Foursome

1. General

In a threesome or a foursome, the partners shall strike off alternately from the teeing grounds, and thereafter shall strike alternately during the play of each hole. Penalty strokes (Def. 24) do not affect the order of play.

2. Match Play

If a player play when his partner should have played, *his side shall lose the hole.*

In a match comprising more than one stipulated round, the partners shall not change the order of striking from the teeing grounds after any stipulated round.

3. Stroke Play

If the partners play a stroke or strokes in incorrect order, such stroke or strokes shall be cancelled, and *the side shall be penalised two strokes.* A ball shall then be put in play as nearly as possible at the spot from which the side first played in incorrect order. This must be done before a stroke has been played from the next teeing ground, or, in the case of the last hole of the round, before the side has left the putting green. If they fail to do so, *they shall be disqualified.* If the first ball was played from the teeing ground, a ball may be teed anywhere within the teeing ground; if from through the green or a hazard, it shall be dropped; if on the putting green, it shall be placed.

Note: *As in stroke play a stipulated round cannot be more than 18 holes (Def. 30), the order of play between partners may be changed for a second or subsequent round, unless the conditions of the competition provide otherwise.*

Rule 16 Ball Played as it Lies

The ball shall be played as it lies, except as otherwise provided for in the Rules or Local Rules.
(Ball at rest moved by player, purposely—Rule 27-1c.)
(Ball at rest moved by player, accidentally—Rule 27-1d.)
(Ball at rest moving accidentally after address—Rule 27-1f.)

Rule 17 Improving Lie or Stance and Influencing Ball Prohibited

1. Improving Line of Play or Lie Prohibited

A player shall not improve, or allow to be improved, his line of play, the position or lie of his ball or the area of his intended swing by moving, bending or breaking anything fixed or growing, or by removing or pressing down sand, loose soil, cut turf placed in position or other irregularities of surface except:—
a. As may occur in the course of fairly taking his stance;
b. In making the stroke or the backward movement of his club for the stroke;
c. On the teeing ground a player may press down irregularities;
d. In repairing damage to the putting green under Rule 35-1c.

The club may be grounded only lightly and must not be pressed on the ground.
(Sand and loose soil on the putting green—Def. 17 and Rule 35-1b.)
(Removal of obstructions—Rule 31-1.)
Note: *Things fixed include objects defining out of bounds.*

2. Long Grass and Bushes

If a ball lie in long grass, rushes, bushes, whins, heather or the like, only so much thereof shall be touched as will enable the player to find and identify his ball; nothing shall be done which may in any way improve its lie.
The player is not of necessity entitled to see the ball when playing a stroke.

3. Building of Stance Prohibited

A player is always entitled to place his feet firmly on the ground when taking his stance, but he is not allowed to build a stance.

4. Exerting Influence on Ball
No player or caddie shall take any action to influence the position or the movement of a ball except in accordance with the Rules.
PENALTY FOR BREACH OF RULE:
Match play—Loss of hole; Stroke play—Two strokes.
Note: *In the case of a serious breach of Rule 17-4, the Committee may impose a penalty of disqualification.*

Rule **18** Loose Impediments *(Def. 17)*

Any loose impediment may be removed without penalty except when both the impediment and the ball lie in or touch a hazard. When a ball is in motion, a loose impediment shall not be removed.
PENALTY FOR BREACH OF RULE:
Match play—Loss of hole; Stroke play—Two strokes.
(Ball moving after loose impediment touched—Rule 27-1e.)
(Finding ball in hazard—Rule 33-1e.)

Rule **19** Striking at Ball

1. Ball to be Fairly Struck at
The ball shall be fairly struck at with the head of the club and must not be pushed, scraped or spooned.
PENALTY FOR BREACH OF RULE 19-1:
Match play—Loss of hole; Stroke play—Two strokes.

2. Striking Ball Twice
If the player strike the ball twice when making a stroke, he shall count the stroke and *add a penalty stroke*, making two strokes in all.
(Playing a moving ball—Rule 25.)

Rule **20** Ball Farther from the Hole Played First

1. General
When the balls are in play, the ball farther from the hole shall be played first. If the balls are equidistant from the hole, the option of playing first should be decided by lot.
A player or a competitor incurs no penalty if a ball is moved in measuring to determine which ball is farther from the hole. A ball so moved shall be replaced.

2. Match Play
Through the green or in a hazard, if a player play when his opponent should have done so, the opponent may immediately require the player to replay the stroke. In such a case, the player shall drop a ball as near as

possible to the spot from which his previous stroke was played, and play in correct order without penalty.

PENALTY FOR BREACH OF RULE 20-2: *Loss of hole.*
(*Playing out of turn on putting green—Rule 35-2b.*)

3. Stroke Play
If a competitor play out of turn, no penalty shall be incurred. The ball shall be played as it lies.

Rule 21 Playing a Wrong Ball (*Def. 5*) or from a Wrong Place

1. General
A player must hole out with the ball driven from the teeing ground unless a Rule or Local Rule permit him to substitute another ball.

2. Match Play
a. Wrong Ball
If a player play a stroke with a wrong ball (Def. 5) except in a hazard, *he shall lose the hole.* There is no penalty if a player play any strokes in a hazard with a wrong ball provided he then play the correct ball; the strokes so played with a wrong ball do not count in the player's score.
If the wrong ball belong to another player, it shall be replaced where it originally lay.
When the player and the opponent exchange balls during the play of a hole, the first to play the wrong ball other than from a hazard shall lose the hole; when this cannot be determined, the hole shall be played out with the balls exchanged.
b. Ball Played from Wrong Place
If a player play a stroke with a ball which has been dropped or placed under an applicable Rule but in a wrong place, *he shall lose the hole.*
Note: *For a ball played outside teeing ground, see Rule 13-1.*

3. Stroke Play
a. Wrong Ball
If a competitor play any strokes with a wrong ball (Def. 5) except in a hazard, *he shall add two penalty strokes* to his score for the hole and shall then play the correct ball. Strokes played by a competitor with a wrong ball do not count in his score. There is no penalty if a competitor play any strokes in a hazard with a wrong ball, provided he then play the correct ball.
If the wrong ball belong to another player, a ball shall be placed where the original ball lay.
b. Rectification After Holing Out
If a competitor hole out with a wrong ball, he may rectify his mistake by proceeding in accordance with Clause 3a of this Rule, subject to the prescribed penalty, provided he has not made a stroke on the next teeing ground, or, in the case of the last hole of the round, has not left the

putting green. *The competitor shall be disqualified* if he does not so rectify his mistake.

c. Ball Played from Wrong Place
If a competitor play a stroke with a ball which has been dropped or placed under an applicable Rule but in a wrong place, *he shall add two penalty strokes* to his score for the hole and shall then play out the hole with that ball.

Note 1: *For a ball played outside teeing ground, see Rule 13-2.*
Note 2: *A serious breach of Rule 21-3c should be dealt with by the Committee under Rule 1.*

Rule 22   Lifting, Dropping and Placing

1. Lifting
A ball to be lifted under the Rules or Local Rules may be lifted by the owner, his partner or either of their caddies, or by another person authorised by the owner. In any such case the owner shall be responsible for any breach of the Rules or Local Rules.
Note: *A referee or observer should not lift a ball or mark its position.* (*Defs. 19 and 26.*)

2. Dropping
a. How to Drop
A ball to be dropped under the Rules or Local Rules shall be dropped by the player himself. He shall face the hole, stand erect, and drop the ball behind him over his shoulder. If a ball be dropped in any other manner and remain the ball in play (Def. 5), *the player shall incur a penalty stroke.*
If the ball touch the player before it strikes the ground, the player shall re-drop without penalty. If the ball touch the player after it strikes the ground or if it come to rest against the player and move when he then moves, there is no penalty, and the ball shall be played as it lies.

b. Where to Drop
When a ball is to be dropped, it shall be dropped as near as possible to the spot where the ball lay, but not nearer the hole, except when a Rule permits it to be dropped elsewhere or placed. In a hazard, the ball must come to rest in that hazard; if it roll out of the hazard, it must be re-dropped, without penalty.

**c. Rolling into Hazard, Out of Bounds, Two Club-lengths
   or Nearer the Hole**
If a dropped ball roll into a hazard, out of bounds, more than two club-lengths from the point where it first struck the ground, or come to rest nearer the hole than its original position, it shall be re-dropped, without penalty. If the ball again roll into such a position, it shall be placed where it first struck the ground when re-dropping.
PENALTY FOR BREACH OF RULE 22-2:
Match play—Loss of hole; Stroke play   Two strokes.

3. Placing

a. How and Where to Place

A ball to be placed or replaced under the Rules or Local Rules shall be placed by the player, his partner or either of their caddies on the spot where the ball lay, except when a Rule permits it to be placed elsewhere.

b. Lie of Ball to be Placed or Replaced Altered

If the original lie of a ball to be placed or replaced has been altered, the ball shall be placed in the nearest lie most similar to that which it originally occupied, not more than two club-lengths from the original lie and not nearer the hole.

c. Spot Not Determinable

If it be impossible to determine the spot where the ball is to be placed, through the green or in a hazard the ball shall be dropped, or on the putting green it shall be placed, as near as possible to the place where it lay, but not nearer the hole.

d. Ball Moving

If a ball when placed fail to remain on the spot on which it was placed, it shall be replaced without penalty. If it still fail to remain on that spot, it shall be placed at the nearest spot not nearer the hole where it can be placed at rest.

PENALTY FOR BREACH OF RULE 22-3:

Match play—Loss of hole; Stroke play—Two strokes.

4. Ball in Play when Dropped or Placed

A ball dropped or placed under a Rule governing the particular case is in play (Def. 5) and shall not be lifted or re-dropped or replaced except as provided in the Rules.

5. Lifting Ball Wrongly Dropped or Placed

A ball dropped or placed but not played may be lifted without penalty if:—

a. It was dropped or placed under a Rule governing the particular case but not in the right place or otherwise not in accordance with that Rule. The player shall then drop or place the ball in accordance with the governing Rule.

b. It was dropped or placed under a Rule which does not govern the particular case. The player shall then proceed under a Rule which governs the case. However, in match play, if, before the opponent plays his next stroke, the player fail to inform him that the ball has been lifted, *the player shall lose the hole.*

Note: *In stroke play a serious breach of Rule 22 should be dealt with by the Committee under Rule 1.*

Rule 23   Identifying or Cleaning Ball

The responsibility for playing the proper ball rests with the player. Each player should put an identification mark on his ball.

1. Identifying Ball

Except in a hazard, the player may, without penalty, lift his ball in play for the purpose of identification and replace it on the spot from which it was lifted provided this is done in the presence of his opponent in match play or marker in stroke play.
(*Touching grass, etc., for identification—Rule 17-2.*)

2. Cleaning Ball

A ball may be cleaned when lifted as follows:—
>From an unplayable lie under Rule 29-2;
>For relief from an obstruction under Rule 31;
>From casual water, ground under repair, or otherwise under Rule 32;
>From a water hazard under Rule 33-2 or 33-3;
>On the putting green under Rule 35-1d or on a wrong putting green under Rule 35-1j.

Otherwise, during the play of a hole a player may not clean a ball, except to the extent necessary for identification or if permitted by Local Rule.
PENALTY FOR BREACH OF RULE:
Match play—Loss of hole; Stroke play—Two strokes.

Rule 24   Ball Interfering with Play

Through the green or in a hazard, a player may have any other ball lifted if he consider that it might interfere with his play. A ball so lifted shall be replaced after the player has played his stroke.
If a ball be accidentally moved in complying with this Rule, no penalty shall be incurred and the ball so moved shall be replaced.
(*Lie of ball to be placed or replaced altered—Rule 22-3b.*)
(*Putting green—Rule 35-2a and 35-3a.*)
PENALTY FOR BREACH OF RULE:
Match play—Loss of hole; Stroke play—Two strokes.

Rule 25   A Moving Ball

1. Playing Moving Ball Prohibited

A player shall not play while his ball is moving.
Exceptions:— Ball falling off tee—Rule 14.
>Striking ball twice—Rule 19-2.
>As herunder—Rule 25-2.

When the ball only begins to move after the player has begun the stroke or the backward movement of his club for the stroke, he shall incur no penalty under this Rule, but he is not exempted from the provisions for:—
Ball at Rest Moved by Player, Accidentally—Rule 27-1d.
Ball at Rest Moving after Loose Impediment Touched—Rule 27-1e.
Ball at Rest Moving Accidentally after Address—Rule 27-1f.

2. Ball Moving in Water

When a ball is in water in a water hazard, the player may, without penalty, make a stroke at it while it is moving, but he must not delay to make his stroke in order to allow the wind or current to better the position of the ball. A ball moving in water in a water hazard may be lifted if the player elect to invoke Rule 33-2 or 33-3.

PENALTY FOR BREACH OF RULE:
Match play—Loss of hole; Stroke play—Two strokes.

Rule 26 Ball in Motion Stopped or Deflected

1. General

a. By Outside Agency
If a ball in motion be accidentally stopped or deflected by any outside agency, it is a rub of the green and the ball shall be played as it lies, without penalty.
Exception:—On putting green—Rule 35-1h.

b. Lodging in Outside Agency
If a ball lodge in any moving outside agency, the player shall, through the green or in a hazard, drop a ball, or on the putting green place a ball, as near as possible to the spot where the object was when the ball lodged in it, without penalty.

2. Match Play

a. By Player
If a player's ball be stopped or deflected by himself, his partner or either of their caddies or equipment, *he shall lose the hole.*

b. By Opponent
If a player's ball be stopped or deflected by an opponent, his caddie or equipment, *the opponent's side shall lose the hole.*
(Ball striking opponent's ball—Rule 27-2b.)
Exception:—Ball striking person attending flagstick—Rule 34-3b.

3. Stroke Play

a. By Competitor
If a competitor's ball be stopped or deflected by himself, his partner or either of their caddies or equipment, *the competitor shall incur a penalty of two strokes.* The ball shall be played as it lies, except when it lodges in the competitor's, his partner's or either of their caddies' clothes or equipment, in which case the competitor shall, through the green or in a hazard, drop the ball, or on the putting green place the ball, as near as possible to where the article was when the ball lodged in it.

b. By Fellow-Competitor
If a competitor's ball be accidentally stopped or deflected by a fellow-competitor, his caddie, ball or equipment, it is a rub of the green and the ball shall be played as it lies.

Exceptions:—
Ball lodging in fellow-competitor's clothes, etc.—Clause 1b of this Rule.
On the putting green, ball striking fellow-competitor's ball in play—Rule 35-3c.
Ball played from putting green stopped or deflected by fellow-competitor, his caddie or equipment—Rule 35-1h.
Ball striking person attending flagstick—Rule 34-3b.
PENALTY FOR BREACH OF RULE:
Match play—Loss of hole; Stroke play—Two strokes.
Note: *If the referee or the Committee determine that a ball has been deliberately stopped or deflected by an outside agency, including a fellow-competitor or his caddie, further procedure should be prescribed in equity under Rule 11-4. On the putting green, Rule 35-1h applies.*

Rule **27**   **Ball at Rest Moved** (*Def. 3*)

1. General
a. By Outside Agency
If a ball at rest be moved by any outside agency, the player shall incur no penalty and shall replace the ball before playing another stroke.
(*Opponent's ball moved by player's ball—Rule 27-2b.*)
Note 1: *Neither wind nor water is an outside agency.*
Note 2: *If the ball moved is not immediately recoverable, another ball may be substituted.*
b. During Search
During search for a ball, if it be moved by an opponent, a fellow-competitor or the equipment or caddie of either, no penalty shall be incurred. The player shall replace the ball before playing another stroke.
c. By Player, Purposely
When a ball is in play, if a player, his partner or either of their caddies purposely move, touch or lift it, except as provided for in the Rules or Local Rules, *the player shall incur a penalty stroke* and the ball shall be replaced. The player may, however, without penalty, touch the ball with his club in the act of addressing it, provided the ball does not move (Def. 3).
d. By Player, Accidentally
When a ball is in play, if a player, his partner, their equipment or either of their caddies accidentally move it, or by touching anything cause it to move, except as provided for in the Rules or Local Rules, *the player shall incur a penalty stroke* and the ball shall be replaced.
(*Ball accidentally moved when measuring to determine which ball farther from the hole—Rule 20-1.*)
(*Ball accidentally moved in the process of marking—Rule 35-2a or 35-3a.*)
e. Ball Moving after Loose Impediment Touched
Through the green, if the ball move before the player has addressed it but after any loose impediment lying within a club-length of it has been touched by the player, his partner or either of their caddies, the player

shall be deemed to have caused the ball to move. *The penalty shall be one stroke*, and the ball shall be replaced.
(*Loose impediment on putting green—Rule 35-1b.*)

f. Ball Moving Accidentally after Address
If a ball in play move after the player has addressed it (Def. 1), he shall be deemed to have caused it to move and *shall incur a penalty stroke*, and the ball shall be played as it lies.

2. Match Play

a. By Opponent
If a player's ball be touched or moved by an opponent, his caddie or equipment (except as otherwise provided in the Rules), *the opponent shall incur a penalty stroke*. The player shall replace the ball before playing another stroke.

b. Opponent's Ball Moved by Player's Ball
If a player's ball move an opponent's ball, no penalty shall be incurred. The opponent may either play his ball as it lies or, before another stroke is played by either side, he may replace the ball.
If the player's ball stop on the spot formerly occupied by the opponent's ball and the opponent declare his intention to replace the ball, the player shall first play another stroke, after which the opponent shall replace his ball.
(*Putting green—Rule 35-2c.*)
(*Three-Ball, Best-Ball and Four-Ball match play—Rule 40-1c.*)

3. Stroke Play

Ball Moved by a Fellow-Competitor
If a competitor's ball be moved by a fellow-competitor, his caddie, ball or equipment, no penalty shall be incurred. The competitor shall replace his ball before playing another stroke.
Exception to Penalty:—Ball striking fellow-competitor's ball on putting green—Rule 35-3c.
PENALTY FOR BREACH OF RULE:
Match play—Loss of hole; *Stroke play—Two strokes.*
(*Playing a wrong ball—Rule 21.*)
Note 1: *If a player who is required to replace a ball fail to do so, the general penalty for a breach of this Rule will apply in addition to any other penalty incurred.*
***Note 2**: A serious breach of this Rule should be dealt with by the Committee under Rule 1.*

Rule 28   Ball Unfit for Play

If the ball become so damaged as to be unfit for play, the player may substitute another ball, placing it on the spot where the original ball lay. Substitution may only be made on the hole during the play of which the damage occurred and in the presence of the opponent in match play or the marker in stroke play.

If a ball break into pieces as a result of a stroke, the stroke shall be replayed, without penalty.

PENALTY FOR BREACH OF RULE:
Match play—Loss of hole; Stroke play—Two strokes.
(Ball unplayable—Rule 29-2.)
Note 1: *Mud or loose impediments adhering to the ball do not make it unfit for play.*
Note 2: *A player is not the sole judge as to whether his ball is unfit for play. If the opponent or the marker dispute a claim of unfitness, the referee, if one is present, or the Committee shall settle the matter (Rule 11-2 or 11-3).*

Rule 29 Ball Lost (*Def. 6*), Out of Bounds (*Def. 21*), or Unplayable

1. Lost or Out of Bounds

a. Procedure
If a ball be lost outside a water hazard or be out of bounds, the player shall play his next stroke as nearly as possible at the spot from which the original ball was played or moved by him, *adding a penalty stroke* to his score for the hole. If the original stroke was played from the teeing ground, a ball may be teed anywhere within the teeing ground; if from through the green or a hazard, it shall be dropped; if on the putting green, it shall be placed.
(Ball lost in casual water, ground under repair, etc.—Rule 32-3.)

b. Ascertaining Location
A player has the right at any time of ascertaining whether his opponent's ball is out of bounds.
A person outside the match may point out the location of a ball for which search is being made.

c. Standing Out of Bounds
A player may stand out of bounds to play a ball lying within bounds.

2. Unplayable

a. Player Sole Judge
The player is the sole judge as to whether his ball is unplayable. It may be declared unplayable at any place on the course except in a water hazard (Rule 33-2 or 33-3).

b. Procedure
If the player deem his ball to be unplayable, he shall either:—
(i) Play his next stroke as provided in Clause 1a of this Rule (*stroke-and-distance penalty*),

or

(ii) Drop a ball, *under penalty of one stroke*, either (a) within two club-lengths of the point where the ball lay, but not nearer the hole, or (b) behind the point where the ball lay, keeping that point between himself and the hole, with no limit to how far behind that

point the ball may be dropped: if the ball lay in a bunker, a ball must be dropped in the bunker.
(*Ball in casual water, etc.—Rule 32.*)
(*Ball unfit for play—Rule 28.*)
PENALTY FOR BREACH OF RULE:
Match play—Loss of hole; *S*troke play—Two strokes.*
*Note: *A serious breach of this Rule should be dealt with by the Committee under Rule 1.*

Rule 30   Provisional Ball (*Def. 5*)

1. Procedure

If a ball may be lost outside a water hazard or may be out of bounds, to save time the player may play another ball provisionally as nearly as possible from the spot at which the original ball was played. If the original ball was played from the teeing ground, the provisional ball may be teed anywhere within the teeing ground; if from through the green or a hazard, it shall be dropped; if on the putting green, it shall be placed.

a. The player must inform his opponent or marker that he intends to play a provisional ball, and he must play it before he or his partner goes forward to search for the original ball: if he fail to do so, and plays another ball, such ball is not a provisional ball and becomes the ball in play *under penalty of stroke and distance* (Rule 29-1); the original ball must be abandoned.

b. Play of a provisional ball from the teeing ground does not affect the order in which the sides play (Rule 12-2).

c. A provisional ball is never an outside agency.

2. Play of a Provisional Ball

a. The player may play a provisional ball until he reaches the place where the original ball is likely to be. If he play any strokes with the provisional ball from a point beyond that place, the original ball is deemed to be lost (Def. 6c).

b. If the original ball be lost outside a water hazard or be out of bounds, the provisional ball becomes the ball in play, *under penalty of stroke and distance* (Rule 29-1).

c. If the original ball be neither lost outside a water hazard nor out of bounds, the player shall abandon the provisional ball and continue play with the original ball. Should he fail to do so, any further strokes played with the provisional ball shall constitute playing a wrong ball and the provisions of Rule 21 shall apply.

PENALTY FOR BREACH OF RULE:
Match play—Loss of hole; Stroke play—Two strokes.
Note: *If the original ball be unplayable or lie or be lost in a water hazard, the player must proceed under Rule 29 2 or Rule 33-2 or 33-3, whichever is applicable.*

Rule 31   Obstructions (*Def. 20*)

1. Movable Obstruction may be Removed

Any movable obstruction may be removed. If the ball be moved in so doing, it shall be replaced on the exact spot from which it was moved, without penalty. If it be impossible to determine the spot or to replace the ball, the player shall proceed in accordance with Rule 22-3.

When a ball is in motion, an obstruction other than an attended flagstick and equipment of the players shall not be removed.

2. Interference by Immovable Obstruction

a. Interference
Interference by an immovable obstruction occurs when the ball lies in or on the obstruction, or so close to the obstruction that the obstruction interferes with the player's stance or the area of his intended swing. The fact that an immovable obstruction intervenes on the line of play is not, of itself, interference under this Rule.

b. Relief
A player may obtain relief from interference by an immovable obstruction, without penalty, as follows:—

(i) *Through the Green:*
Through the green, the nearest point shall be determined (without crossing over, through or under the obstruction) which (a) is not nearer the hole, (b) avoids interference as defined in Clause 2a of this Rule, and (c) is not in a hazard or on a putting green. He shall lift the ball and drop it within two club-lengths of the point thus determined on ground which fulfils (a), (b) and (c) above.
Note: *The prohibition against crossing over, through or under the obstruction does not apply to the artificial surfaces and sides of roads and paths or when the ball lies in or on the obstruction.*

(ii) *In a Hazard:*
In a hazard, the player may lift and drop the ball in accordance with Clause (i) above, but the ball must be dropped in the hazard.

(iii) *On the Putting Green:*
On the putting green, the player may lift and place the ball in the nearest position to where it lay which affords relief from interference, but not nearer the hole.

c. Re-dropping
If a dropped ball roll into a position covered by this Rule, or nearer the hole than its original position, it shall be re-dropped without penalty. If it again roll into such a position, it shall be placed where it first struck the ground when re-dropped.

PENALTY FOR BREACH OF RULE:
Match play—Loss of hole; Stroke play—Two strokes.

Rule 32 Casual Water (*Def. 8*), Ground Under Repair (*Def. 13*), Hole Made by Burrowing Animal

1. Interference

Interference by casual water, ground under repair, or a hole, cast or runway made by a burrowing animal, a reptile or a bird occurs when a ball lies in or touches any of these conditions or when the condition interferes with the player's stance or the area of his intended swing. If interference exists, the player may either play the ball as it lies or take relief as provided in Clause 2 of this Rule.

2. Relief

If the player elect to take relief, he shall proceed as follows:—

a. Through the Green

Through the green, the nearest point shall be determined which (a) is not nearer the hole, (b) avoids interference by the condition, and (c) is not in a hazard or on a putting green. The player shall lift the ball and drop it without penalty within two club-lengths of the point thus determined on ground which fulfils (a), (b) and (c) above.

b. In a Hazard

In a hazard, the player shall lift and drop the ball either:—

Without penalty, in the hazard as near as possible to the spot where the ball lay, but not nearer the hole, on ground which affords maximum relief from the condition;

or

Under penalty of one stroke, outside the hazard, but not nearer the hole, keeping the spot where the ball lay between himself and the hole.

c. On the Putting Green

On the putting green, or if such condition on the putting green intervene between a ball lying on the putting green and the hole, the player shall lift the ball and place it without penalty in the nearest position to where it lay which affords maximum relief from the condition, but not nearer the hole nor in a hazard.

3. Ball Lost

a. Outside a Hazard

If a ball be lost under a condition covered by this Rule, except in a hazard, the player may take relief as follows: the nearest point to the spot where the ball last crossed the margin of the area shall be determined which (a) is not nearer the hole than where the ball last crossed that margin, (b) avoids interference by the condition, and (c) is not in a hazard or on a putting green. He shall drop a ball without penalty within two club-lengths of the point thus determined on ground which fulfils (a), (b) and (c) above.

b. In a Hazard
If a ball be lost in a hazard under a condition covered by this Rule, the player may drop a ball either:—
Without penalty, in the hazard, but not nearer the hole than the spot at which the ball last crossed the margin of the area, on ground which affords maximum relief from the condition;
or
Under penalty of one stroke, outside the hazard, but not nearer the hole, keeping the spot at which the ball last crossed the margin of the hazard between himself and the hole.
In order that a ball may be treated as lost under a condition covered by this Rule, there must be reasonable evidence to that effect.

4. Re-Dropping
If a dropped ball roll into the area from which relief was taken, or come to rest in such a position that that area still affects the player's stance or the area of his intended swing, the ball shall be re-dropped, without penalty. If the ball again roll into such a position, it shall be placed where it first struck the ground when re-dropped.
PENALTY FOR BREACH OF RULE:
Match play—Loss of hole; Stroke play—Two strokes.

Rule 33   Hazards (*Def. 14*)

1. Touching Hazard Prohibited
When a ball lies in or touches a hazard or a water hazard, nothing shall be done which may in any way improve its lie. Before making a stroke, the player shall not touch the ground in the hazard or water in the water hazard with a club or otherwise, nor touch or move a loose impediment lying in or touching the hazard, nor test the condition of the hazard or of any similar hazard; subject to the following considerations:—
a. Stance
The player may place his feet firmly in taking his stance.
b. Touching Fixed or Growing Object
In addressing the ball or in the stroke or in the backward movement for the stroke, the club may touch any wooden or stone wall, paling or similar fixed object or any grass, bush, tree, or other growing substance (but the club may not be soled in the hazard).
c. Obstructions
The player is entitled to relief from obstructions under the provisions of Rule 31.
d. Loose Impediment Outside Hazard
Any loose impediment not in or touching the hazard may be removed.
e. Finding Ball
If the ball be covered by sand, fallen leaves or the like, the player may remove as much thereof as will enable him to see the top of the ball. If the ball be moved in such removal, no penalty shall be incurred, and the ball shall be replaced.

If the ball is believed to be lying in water in a water hazard, the player may probe for it with a club or otherwise. If the ball be moved in such search, no penalty shall be incurred; the ball shall be replaced, unless the player elects to proceed under Clause 2 or 3 of this Rule. The ball may not be lifted for identification.

f. Placing Clubs in Hazard
The player may, without penalty, place his clubs in the hazard prior to making a stroke, provided nothing is done which may improve the lie of the ball or constitute testing the soil.

g. Smoothing Irregularities
There is no penalty should soil or sand in the hazard be smoothed by the player after playing a stroke, or by his caddie at any time without the authority of the player, provided nothing is done that improves the lie of the ball or assists the player in his subsequent play of the hole.

h. Casual Water, Ground under Repair
The player is entitled to relief from casual water, ground under repair, and otherwise as provided for in Rule 32.

i. Interference by a Ball
The player is entitled to relief from interference by another ball under the provisions of Rule 24.

2. Ball in Water Hazard (*Def. 14b*)

If a ball lie or be lost in a water hazard (whether the ball lie in water or not), the player may drop a ball, *under penalty of one stroke*, either:—
a. Behind the water hazard, keeping the spot at which the ball last crossed the margin of the water hazard between himself and the hole, and with no limit to how far behind the water hazard the ball may be dropped,

or

b. As near as possible to the spot from which the original ball was played; if the stroke was played from the teeing ground, the ball may be teed anywhere within the teeing ground.

Note: *If a ball has been played from within a water hazard and has not crossed any margin of the hazard, the player may drop a ball behind the hazard under Rule 33-2a.*

3. Ball in Lateral Water Hazard (*Def. 14c*)

If a ball lie or be lost in a lateral water hazard, the player may, *under penalty of one stroke*, either:—
a. Play his next stroke in accordance with Clause 2a or 2b of this Rule,

or

b. Drop a ball outside the hazard within two club-lengths of the point where the ball last crossed the margin of the hazard or a point on the opposite margin of the hazard equidistant from the hole. The dropped ball must come to rest not nearer the hole than the point where the original ball last crossed the margin of the hazard.

Note: *If a ball has been played from within a lateral water hazard and has not crossed any margin of the hazard, the player may drop a ball outside the hazard under Rule 33-3b.*

PENALTY FOR BREACH OF RULE:
Match play—Loss of hole; *Stroke play—Two strokes.*
***Note 1:** A serious breach of this Rule should be dealt with by the Committee under Rule 1.*
Note 2: *It is a question of fact whether a ball lost after having been struck toward a water hazard is lost inside or outside the hazard. In order to treat the ball as lost in the hazard, there must be reasonable evidence that the ball lodged therein. In the absence of such evidence, the ball must be treated as a lost ball and Rule 29-1 applies.*

Rule 34   The Flagstick (*Def. 12*)

1. Flagstick Attended, Removed or Held Up
Before and during the stroke, the player may have the flagstick attended, removed or held up to indicate the position of the hole. This may be done only on the authority of the player before he plays his stroke. If the flagstick be attended or removed by an opponent, a fellow-competitor or the caddie of either with the knowledge of the player and no objection is made, the player shall be deemed to have authorised it.
If a player or a caddie attend or remove the flagstick or stand near the hole while a stroke is being played, he shall be deemed to attend the flagstick until the ball comes to rest.
If the flagstick be not attended before the stroke is played, it shall not be attended or removed while the ball is in motion.

2. Unauthorised Attendance
a. Match Play
In match play, an opponent or his caddie shall not attend or remove the flagstick without the knowledge or authority of the player.
b. Stroke Play
In stroke play, if a fellow-competitor or his caddie attend or remove the flagstick without the knowledge or authority of the competitor, and if the ball strike the flagstick or the person attending it, it is a rub of the green, there is no penalty, and the ball shall be played as it lies.
PENALTY FOR BREACH OF RULE 34-1 AND 34-2:
Match play—Loss of hole; Stroke play—Two strokes.

3. Ball Striking Flagstick or Attendant
The player's ball shall not strike either:—
a. The flagstick when attended or removed by the player, his partner or either of their caddies, or by another person with the knowledge or authority of the player; or
b. The player's caddie, his partner or his partner's caddie when attending the flagstick, or another person attending the flagstick with the knowledge or authority of the player, or equipment carried by any such person; or
c. The flagstick in the hole, unattended, when the ball has been played from the putting green.

PENALTY FOR BREACH OF RULE 34-3:
Match play—Loss of hole; Stroke play—Two strokes, and the ball shall be played as it lies.

4. Ball Resting Against Flagstick

If the ball rest against the flagstick when it is in the hole, the player shall be entitled to have the flagstick removed, and if the ball fall into the hole the player shall be deemed to have holed out at his last stroke; otherwise, the ball shall be placed on the lip of the hole, without penalty.
Note: *A referee, observer, marker, steward, gallery marshal or other outside agency should not attend the flagstick.*

Rule 35 The Putting Green (*Def. 25*)

1. General

a. Touching Line of Putt

The line of the putt must not be touched except as provided in Clauses 1b, 1c and 1d of this Rule, or in measuring (Rule 20-1), but the player may place the club in front of the ball in addressing it without pressing anything down.

b. Loose Impediments

The player may move sand, loose soil or any loose impediments on the putting green by picking them up or brushing them aside with his hand or a club without pressing anything down. If the ball be moved, it shall be replaced, without penalty.

c. Repair of Ball Marks

The player may repair damage to the putting green caused by the impact of a ball. If the player's ball lie on the putting green, it may be lifted to permit repair and shall be replaced on the spot from which it was lifted; in match play the ball must be replaced immediately if the opponent so requests.
If a ball be moved during such repair, it shall be replaced, without penalty.

d. Lifting and Cleaning Ball

A ball lying on the putting green may be lifted, without penalty, cleaned if desired and replaced on the spot from which it was lifted; in match play the ball must be replaced immediately if the opponent so requests.

e. Direction for Putting

When the player's ball is on the putting green, the player's caddie, his partner or his partner's caddie may, before the stroke is played, point out a line for putting, but the line of the putt shall not be touched in front of, to the side of, or behind the hole.
While making the stroke, the player shall not allow his caddie, his partner, or his partner's caddie to position himself on or close to an extension of the line·of putt behind the ball.
No mark shall be placed anywhere on the putting green to indicate a line for putting.

f. Testing Surface
During the play of a hole, a player shall not test the surface of the putting green by rolling a ball or roughening or scraping the surface.

g. Other Ball to be at Rest
While the player's ball is in motion after a stroke on the putting green, an opponent's or a fellow-competitor's ball shall not be played or touched.

h. Ball in Motion Stopped or Deflected
If a ball in motion after a stroke on the putting green be stopped or deflected by any moving or animate outside agency, the stroke shall be cancelled and the ball shall be replaced.

Note: *If the referee or the Committee determine that a ball has been deliberately stopped or deflected by an outside agency, including a fellow-competitor or his caddie, further procedure should be prescribed in equity under Rule 11-4.*

i. Ball Overhanging Hole
When any part of the ball overhangs the edge of the hole, the owner of the ball is not allowed more than a few seconds to determine whether it is at rest. If by then the ball has not fallen into the hole, it is deemed to be at rest.

j. Ball on a Wrong Putting Green
If a ball lie on a putting green other than that of the hole being played, the nearest point shall be determined which (a) is not nearer the hole and (b) is not in a hazard or on a putting green. The player shall lift the ball and drop it without penalty within two club-lengths of the point thus determined on ground which fulfils (a) and (b) above.

Note: *Unless otherwise stipulated by the Committee, the term "a putting green other than that of the hole being played" includes a practice putting or pitching green lying within the boundaries of the course.*

k. Ball to be Marked when Lifted
When a ball on the putting green is to be lifted, its position shall be marked.
(Lifting and placing—Rule 22.)

Note: *The position of a lifted ball should be marked by placing a ball-marker or other small object on the putting green, immediately behind the ball. If the marker interfere with the play, stance or stroke of another player, it should be placed one or more putterhead-lengths to one side.*

L. Standing Astride or on Line of Putt Prohibited
The player shall not make a stroke on the putting green from a stance, astride, or with either foot touching, the line of the putt or an extension of that line behind the ball. For the purpose of Rule 35-1L only, the line of putt does not extend beyond the hole.

PENALTY FOR BREACH OF RULE 35-1:
Match play—Loss of hole; Stroke play—Two strokes.

2. Match Play

a. Ball Interfering with Play
When the ball nearer the hole lies on the putting green, if the player consider that the opponent's ball might either be struck by his ball or

interfere with his stance or stroke, the player may require the opponent to lift his ball. The opponent shall replace his ball after the player has played his stroke. If the player's ball stop on the spot formerly occupied by the lifted ball, the player shall first play another stroke before the lifted ball is replaced.

If a ball be accidentally moved in complying with this Rule, no penalty shall be incurred and the ball shall be replaced.

b. Playing Out of Turn

If a player play when his opponent should have done so, the opponent may immediately require the player to replay the stroke, in which case the player shall replace his ball and play in correct order, without penalty.

c. Opponent's Ball Displaced

If the player's ball knock the opponent's ball into the hole, the opponent shall be deemed to have holed out at his last stroke.

If the player's ball move the opponent's ball, the opponent may replace it, but this must be done before another stroke is played by either side. If the player's ball stop on the spot formerly occupied by the opponent's ball, and the opponent declare his intention to replace his ball, the player shall first play another stroke, after which the opponent shall replace his ball.

(*Three-Ball, Best-Ball and Four-Ball match play—Rule 40-1c.*)

d. Conceding Opponent's Next Stroke

When the opponent's ball has come to rest, the player may concede the opponent to have holed out with his next stroke and may remove the opponent's ball with a club or otherwise. If the player does not concede the opponent's next stroke and the opponent's ball fall into the hole, the opponent shall be deemed to have holed out with his last stroke.

If the opponent's next stroke has not been conceded, the opponent shall play without delay in correct order.

PENALTY FOR BREACH OF RULE 35-2: *Loss of hole.*

3. Stroke Play

a. Ball Interfering with Play

When the ball nearer the hole lies on the putting green, if the competitor consider that the fellow-competitor's ball might either be struck by his ball or interfere with his stance or stroke, the competitor may require the fellow-competitor to lift or play his ball, at the option of its owner, without penalty.

If a ball be accidentally moved in the process of marking, lifting or replacing, no penalty shall be incurred and the ball so moved shall be replaced.

If the owner of the ball refuse to comply with this Rule when required to do so, the competitor making the request may lift the ball, *and the owner of the ball shall be disqualified.*

Note: *It is recommended that the ball nearer the hole be played, rather than lifted, unless the subsequent play of a fellow-competitor is likely to be affected.*

b. Ball Assisting Play

If the fellow-competitor consider that his ball lying on the putting green might be of assistance to the competitor, the fellow-competitor may lift or play first, without penalty.

c. Ball Striking Fellow-Competitor's Ball
When both balls lie on the putting green, if the competitor's ball strike a fellow-competitor's ball, *the competitor shall incur a penalty of two strokes* and shall play his ball as it lies. The fellow-competitor's ball shall be at once replaced.

d. Ball Lifted Before Holed Out
For ball lifted before holed out, see Rule 7-3 and Rule 27-1c.

Rule 36 The Committee (*Def. 9*)

1. Conditions
The Committee shall lay down the conditions under which a competition is to be played.

Certain special rules governing stroke play are so substantially different from those governing match play that combining the two forms of play is not practicable and is not permitted. The results of matches played and the scores returned in these circumstances shall not be accepted.

2. Order and Times of Starting
a. General
The Committee shall arrange the order and times of starting.

b. Match Play
When a competition is played over an extended period, the Committee shall lay down the limit of time within which each round shall be completed.

When players are allowed to arrange the date of their match within these limits, the Committee should announce that the match must be played at a stated hour on the last day of the period unless the players agree to a prior date.

c. Stroke Play
Competitors shall play in couples unless the Committee authorises play by threes or fours. If there be a single competitor, the Committee shall provide him with a player who shall mark for him, or provide a marker and allow him to compete alone, or allow him to compete with another group.

3. Decision of Ties
The Committee shall announce the manner, day and time for the decision of a halved match or of a tie, whether played on level terms or under handicap.

A halved match shall not be decided by stroke play. A tie in stroke play shall not be decided by a match.

4. The Course
a. New Holes
New holes should be made on the day on which a stroke competition

begins, and at such other times as the Committee considers necessary, provided all competitors in a single round play with each hole cut in the same position.

b. Practice Ground

Where there is no practice ground available outside the area of a competition course, the Committee should lay down the area on which players may practise on any day of a competition, if it is practicable to do so. On any day of a stroke competition, the Committee should not normally permit practice on or to a putting green or from a hazard of the competition course.

c. Course Unplayable

If the Committee or its authorised representative consider that for any reason the course is not in a playable condition, or that there are circumstances which render the proper playing of the game impossible, it shall have the power in match and stroke play to order a temporary suspension of play, or in stroke play to declare play null and void and to cancel all scores for the round in question.

When a round is cancelled, all penalties incurred in that round are cancelled.

When play has been temporarily suspended, it shall be resumed from where it was discontinued, even though resumption occur on a subsequent day.

(*Procedure in discontinuing play—Rule 37-6b.*)

5. Modification of Penalty

The Committee has no power to waive a Rule of Golf. A penalty of disqualification, however, may, in exceptional individual cases, be waived or be modified or be imposed under Rule 1 if the Committee consider such action warranted.

6. Defining Bounds and Margins

The Committee shall define accurately:—
a. The course and out of bounds.
b. The margins of hazards, water hazards, and lateral water hazards, where there is any doubt.
c. Ground under repair.
d. Obstructions.

7. Local Rules

a. Policy

The Committee shall make and publish Local Rules for abnormal conditions, having regard to the policy of the Governing Authority of the country concerned as set forth in Appendix I attached to these Rules.

b. Waiving Penalty Prohibited

A penalty imposed by a Rule of Golf shall not be waived by a Local Rule.

Rule 37   The Player

1. Conditions
The player shall be responsible for acquainting himself with the conditions under which the competition is to be played.

2. Caddie and Forecaddie
For any breach of a Rule or Local Rule by his caddie, the player incurs the relative penalty.
The player may have only one caddie, *under penalty of disqualification*.
The player may send his own caddie forward to mark the position of any ball.
If a forecaddie be employed by the Committee, he is an outside agency (Def. 22).

3. Infringement Assisting Partner
If a player's infringement of a Rule or Local Rule assist his partner's play, *the partner incurs the relative penalty in addition to any penalty incurred by the player.*

4. Handicap
Before starting in a handicap competition, the player shall ensure that his current handicap is recorded correctly on the official list, if any, for the competition and on the card issued for him by the Committee. In the case of match play or bogey, par or Stableford competitions, he shall inform himself of the holes at which strokes are given or taken.
If a player play off a higher handicap than his current one, *he shall be disqualified* from the handicap competition. If he play off a lower one, the score, or the result of the match, shall stand.

5. Time and Order of Starting
The player shall start at the time and in the order arranged by the Committee.
PENALTY FOR BREACH OF RULE 37-5: *Disqualification.*

6. Discontinuance of Play
a. When Permitted
The player shall not discontinue play on account of bad weather or for any other reason, unless:—
He considers that there be danger from lightning,
or
There be some other reason, such as sudden illness, which the Committee considers satisfactory.
If the player discontinue play without specific permission from the Committee, he shall report to the Committee as soon as possible.

General Exception:—Players discontinuing match play by agreement are not subject to disqualification unless by so doing the competition is delayed.

PENALTY FOR BREACH OF RULE 37-6a: *Disqualification.*

b. Procedure

When play is discontinued in accordance with the Rules, it should, if feasible, be discontinued after the completion of the play of a hole. If this is not feasible, the player should lift his ball after marking the spot on which it lay; in such case he shall replace the ball on that spot when play is resumed.

PENALTY FOR BREACH OF RULE 37-6b:

Match play—Loss of hole; *Stroke play—Two strokes.*

*****Note**: *A serious breach of this Rule should be dealt with by the Committee under Rule 1.*

7. Undue Delay

The player shall at all times play without undue delay. Between the completion of a hole and driving off the next tee, the player may not delay play in any way.

PENALTY FOR BREACH OF RULE 37-7:

**Match play—Loss of hole; Stroke play—Two strokes.*

For repeated offence—Disqualification.

If the player delay play between holes, he is delaying the play of the next hole, and the penalty applies to that hole.

8. Refusal to Comply with Rule

If a competitor in stroke play refuse to comply with a Rule affecting the rights of another competitor, *he shall be disqualified.*

9. Artificial Devices

Except as provided for under the Rules, the player shall not use any artificial device:—

a. Which might assist him in making a stroke or in his play;

b. For the purpose of gauging or measuring distance or conditions which might affect his play; *or*

c. Which, not being part of the grip (see Appendix IId), is designed to give him artificial aid in gripping the club.

(*Exceptions to Rule 37-9c:* Plain gloves and material or substance applied to the grip, such as tape, gauze or resin.)

PENALTY FOR BREACH OF RULE 37-9: *Disqualification.*

Rule 38   Scoring in Stroke Play

1. Recording Scores

The Committee shall issue for each competitor a score card containing the date and the competitor's name.

After each hole the marker shall check the score with the competitor. On completion of the round the marker shall sign the card and hand it to the competitor; should more than one marker record the scores, each shall sign the part for which he is responsible.

2. Checking Scores

The competitor shall check his score for each hole, settle any doubtful points with the Committee, ensure that the marker has signed the card, countersign the card himself, and return it to the Committee as soon as possible. The competitor is solely responsible for the correctness of the score recorded for each hole.

PENALTY FOR BREACH OF RULE 38-2: *Disqualification.*

The Committee is responsible for the addition of scores and application of the handicap recorded on the card.

Exception: Four-ball stroke play—Rule 41-1d.

3. No Alteration of Scores

No alteration may be made on a card after the competitor has returned it to the Committee.

If the competitor return a score for any hole lower than actually played, *he shall be disqualified.*

A score higher than actually played must stand as returned.

Exception:—Four-ball stroke play—Rule 41-8a.

Rule 39 Bogey, Par or Stableford Competitions

1. Conditions

A bogey, par or Stableford competition is a form of stroke competition in which play is against a fixed score at each hole of the stipulated round or rounds.

a. The reckoning for bogey or par competitions is made as in match play. The winner is the competitor who is most successful in the aggregate of holes.

b. The reckoning in Stableford competitions is made by points awarded in relation to a fixed score at each hole as follows:—

For hole done in one over fixed score	1 point
For hole done in fixed score	2 points
For hole done in one under fixed score	3 points
For hole done in two under fixed score	4 points
For hole done in three under fixed score	5 points

The winner is the competitor who scores the highest number of points.

2. Rules for Stroke Play Apply

The Rules for stroke play shall apply with the following modifications:—

a. No Return at any Hole

Any hole for which a competitor makes no return shall be regarded as a loss in bogey and par competitions and as scoring no points in Stableford competitions.

b. Scoring Cards
The holes at which strokes are to be given or taken shall be indicated on the card issued by the Committee.

c. Recording Scores
In bogey and par competitions the marker shall be responsible for marking only the gross number of strokes for each hole where the competitor makes a net score equal to or less than the fixed score. In Stableford competitions the marker shall be responsible for marking only the gross number of strokes at each hole where the competitor's net score earns one or more points.

Note: *Maximum of 14 Clubs—see Rule 3-2 and Rule 41-7.*

3. Disqualification Penalties

a. From the Competition
A competitor shall be disqualified from the competition for a breach of any of the following:

Rule 2—The Club and the Ball.
Rule 4—Agreement to Waive Rules Prohibited.
Rule 8-3—Practice before Round.
Rule 35-3a—Putting Green: Stroke Play, Ball Interfering with Play.
Rule 37-2—Caddie and Forecaddie.
Rule 37-5—Time and Order of Starting.
Rule 37-6a—Discontinuance of Play.
Rule 37-7—Undue Delay (repeated offence).
Rule 37-8—Refusal to Comply with Rule.
Rule 37-9—Artificial Devices.
Rule 38-2—Checking Scores.
Rule 38-3—No Alteration of Scores, except that the competitor shall not be disqualified when a breach of this Rule does not affect the result of the hole.

b. For a Hole
In all other cases where a breach of a Rule would entail disqualification, *the competitor shall be disqualified only for the hole at which the breach occurred.*
(*Modification of penalty—Rule 36-5.*)

Rule 40   Three-Ball, Best-Ball and Four-Ball Match Play

1. General

a. Rules of Golf Apply
The Rules of Golf, so far as they are not at variance with the following special Rules, shall apply to all three-ball, best-ball and four-ball matches.

b. Ball Influencing Play
Any player may have any ball (except the ball about to be played) lifted

if he consider that it might interfere with or be of assistance to a player or side, but this may not be done while any ball in the match is in motion.

c. Ball Moved by Another Ball
There is no penalty if a player's ball move any other ball in the match. The owner of the moved ball shall replace his ball.

d. Playing out of Turn
Through the green or in a hazard, a player shall incur no penalty if he play when an opponent should have done so. The stroke shall not be replayed.

On the putting green, if a player play when an opponent should have done so, the opponent may immediately require the player to replay the stroke in correct order, without penalty.

2. Three-Ball Match Play
In a three-ball match, each player is playing two distinct matches.

a. Ball Stopped or Deflected by an Opponent
If a player's ball be stopped or deflected by an opponent, his caddie or equipment, *that opponent shall lose the hole in his match with the player.* The other opponent shall treat the occurrence as a rub of the green (Def. 27).
Exception:—Ball striking person attending flagstick—Rule 34-3b.

b. Ball at Rest Moved by an Opponent
If the player's ball be touched or moved by an opponent, his caddie or equipment (except as otherwise provided in the Rules), Rule 27-2a applies. *That opponent shall incur a penalty stroke in his match with the player,* but not in his match with the other opponent.

3. Best-Ball and Four-Ball Match Play

a. Order of Play
Balls belonging to the same side may be played in the order the side considers best.

b. Ball Stopped by Player's Side
If a player's ball be stopped or deflected by the player, his partner or either of their caddies or equipment, *the player is disqualified for the hole.* His partner incurs no penalty.

c. Ball Stopped by Opponent's Side
If a player's ball be stopped or deflected by an opponent, his caddie or equipment, *the opponent's side shall lose the hole.*
Exception:—Ball striking person attending flagstick—Rule 34-3b.

d. Wrong Ball
If a player play a stroke with a wrong ball (Def. 5) except in a hazard, *he shall be disqualified for that hole,* but the penalty shall not apply to his partner. If the wrong ball be a ball in the match, its owner shall place a ball on the spot from which the wrong ball was played.

e. Partner's Ball Moved by Player Accidentally
If a player, his partner, or either of their caddies accidentally move a ball owned by their side or by touching anything cause it to move (except as otherwise provided for in the Rules), *the owner of the ball shall incur a*

penalty stroke, but the penalty shall not apply to his partner. The ball shall be replaced.

f. Ball Moved by Opponent's Side

If a player's ball be touched or moved by an opponent, his caddie or equipment (except as otherwise provided for in the Rules), *that opponent shall incur a penalty stroke*, but the penalty shall not apply to the other opponent. The player shall replace the ball, without penalty.

g. Maximum of Fourteen Clubs

The side shall be penalised for a violation of Rule 3 by either partner.

h. Disqualification Penalties

A player shall be disqualified from the match for a breach of Rule 37-5 (Time and Order of Starting), but, in the discretion of the Committee, the penalty shall not necessarily apply to his partner (Def. 28—Note).

A side shall be disqualified for a breach of any of the following:—

    Rule 2—The Club and the Ball.

    Rule 4—Agreement to Waive Rules Prohibited.

    Rule 37-2—Caddie and Forecaddie.

    Rule 37-7—Undue Delay (repeated offence).

    Rule 37-9—Artificial Devices.

A player shall be disqualified for the hole in question and from the remainder of the match for a breach of Rule 37-6a (Discontinuance of Play), but the penalty shall not apply to his partner.

(*Modification of penalty—Rule 36-5.*)

i. Infringement Assisting Partner or Affecting Opponent

If a player's infringement of a Rule or Local Rule assist his partner's play or adversely affect an opponent's play, *the partner incurs the relative penalty in addition to any penalty incurred by the player.*

j. Penalty Applies to Player Only

In all other cases where, by the Rules of Golf, a player would incur a penalty, the penalty shall not apply to his partner.

k. Another Form of Match Played Concurrently

In a best-ball or a four-ball match when another form of match is played concurrently, the above special Rules shall apply.

Rule 41   Four-Ball Stroke Play

1. Conditions

a. The Rules of Golf, so far as they are not at variance with the following special Rules, shall apply to four-ball stroke play.

b. In four-ball stroke play two competitors play as partners, each playing his own ball.

c. The lower score of the partners is the score of the hole.

If one partner fail to complete the play of a hole, there is no penalty.

(*Wrong score—Rule 41-8a.*)

d. The marker is required to record for each hole only the gross score of whichever partner's score is to count. The partners are responsible for the correctness of only their gross scores for each hole. The Committee is responsible for recording the better-ball score for each hole, the addition and the application of the handicaps recorded on the card.

e. Only one of the partners need be responsible for complying with Rule 38.

2. Ball Influencing Play

Any competitor may have any ball (except the ball about to be played) lifted or played, at the option of the owner, if he consider that it might interfere with or be of assistance to a competitor or side, but this may not be done while any ball in the group is in motion.

If the owner of the ball refuse to comply with this Rule when required to do so, *his side shall be disqualified.*

3. Balls to be at Rest

While the competitor's ball is in motion after a stroke on the putting green, any other ball shall not be played or touched.

4. Ball Struck by Another Ball

When the balls concerned lie on the putting green, if a competitor's ball strike any other ball, *the competitor shall incur a penalty of two strokes* and shall play his ball as it lies. The other ball shall be at once replaced.

In all other cases, if a competitor's ball strike any other ball, the competitor shall play his ball as it lies. The owner of the moved ball shall replace his ball, without penalty.

5. Order of Play

Balls belonging to the same side may be played in the order the side considers best.

6. Wrong Ball

If a competitor play any strokes with a wrong ball (Def. 5) except in a hazard, *he shall add two penalty strokes* to his score for the hole and then play the correct ball (Rule 21-3).

If the wrong ball be a ball in the competition, its owner shall place a ball on the spot from which the wrong ball was played.

7. Maximum of Fourteen Clubs

The side shall be penalised for a violation of Rule 3 by either partner.

8. Disqualification Penalties

a. From the Competition

A competitor shall be disqualified from the competition for a breach of any of the following, but the penalty shall not apply to his partner:—

Rule 8-3—Practice before Round.

Rule 37-5—Time and Order of Starting.

A side shall be disqualified from the competition for a breach of any of the following:—

Rule 2—The Club and the Ball.
Rule 4—Agreement to Waive Rules Prohibited.
Rule 37-2—Caddie and Forecaddie.
Rule 37-7—Undue Delay (repeated offence).
Rule 37-8—Refusal to Comply with Rule.
Rule 37-9—Artificial Devices.
Rule 38-2—Checking Scores.
Rule 38-3—No Alteration of Scores, i.e. when the recorded lower score of the partners is lower than actually played. If the recorded lower score of the partners is higher than actually played, it must stand as returned.
Rule 41-2—Ball Influencing Play, Refusal to Lift.
By both partners, at the same hole, of a Rule or Rules the penalty for which is disqualification either from the competition or for a hole.

b. From the Remainder of the Competition
A competitor shall be disqualified for the hole in question and from the remainder of the competition for a breach of Rule 37-6a (Discontinuance of Play), but the penalty shall not apply to his partner.

c. For the Hole Only
In all other cases where a breach of a Rule would entail disqualification, *the competitor shall be disqualified only for the hole at which the breach occurred.*
(*Modification of penalty—Rule 36-5.*)

9. Infringement Assisting Partner

If a competitor's infringement of a Rule or Local Rule assist his partner's play, *the partner incurs the relative penalty in addition to any penalty incurred by the competitor.*

10. Penalty Applies to Competitor Only

In all other cases where, by the Rules of Golf, a competitor would incur a penalty, the penalty shall not apply to his partner.

Appendix I Local Rules

Committees in charge of courses shall, when considered necessary,
1. Make Local Rules for such abnormal conditions as:—
a. Existence of mud.
b. Accumulation of leaves.
c. Unusual damage to course.
d. Stones in bunkers.
e. Other local conditions which could be held to interfere with the proper playing of the Game. If this necessitates modification of a Rule of Golf the approval of the Governing Authority must be obtained.
f. Conditions which make a Local Rule necessary for the preservation of the course; this includes prohibition, where necessary, of playing a ball lying in ground under repair.

g. Obstructions, their limits and the extent of relief if the application of Rule 31 is impracticable or inequitable.

h. Any construction which the Committee considers an integral part of the course (Def. 20c), and defines as not an obstruction.

i. Subject to the approval of the Governing Authority, permitting play of a provisional ball for a ball which may be in a water hazard of such character that it would be impracticable to determine whether the ball is in the hazard or to do so would unduly delay play.

Note: *The play of a provisional ball will automatically disallow the procedure under Rule 33-2 or 33-3.*

2. Frame regulations governing Priority on the Course.

3. Frame regulations governing practice during stroke competitions. (Rules 8-3, 36-4b.)

Appendix II **Design of Clubs** (*Def. 36*)

Rule 2-2a provides in part:

"The golf club shall be composed of a shaft and a head, and all of the various parts shall be fixed so that the club is one unit; the club shall not be designed to be adjustable, except for weight.

Note: Playing characteristics not to be changed during a round—Rule 2-2b.

The club shall not be substantially different from the traditional and customary form and make, and shall conform with the regulations governing the design of clubs."

The following are the regulations governing the design of clubs:—

a. Shape of Head

The length of a clubhead shall be greater than the breadth.

Length shall be determined on a horizontal line, 0·625 inches (16 mm) above the sole, from the back of the heel to the end of the toe or a vertical projection thereof.

Breadth shall be determined on a horizontal line between the outermost points of the face and the back of the head or vertical projections thereof.

b. Face of Head

The club shall have only one face designed for striking the ball, except that a putter may have two faces if the loft of both faces is substantially the same and does not exceed ten degrees.

Club faces shall not embody any degree of concavity on the hitting surface.

Club faces shall not have any lines, dots or other markings with sharp or rough edges, or any type of finish, for the purpose of unduly influencing the movement of the ball.

Markings on the face of a club shall conform with the specifications in Appendix III at pages 77 to 81.

The face of an iron club shall not contain an inset or attachment.

c. Shaft

The shaft shall be designed to be straight from the top to a point not more than 5 inches (127 mm) above the sole. The shaft, including any

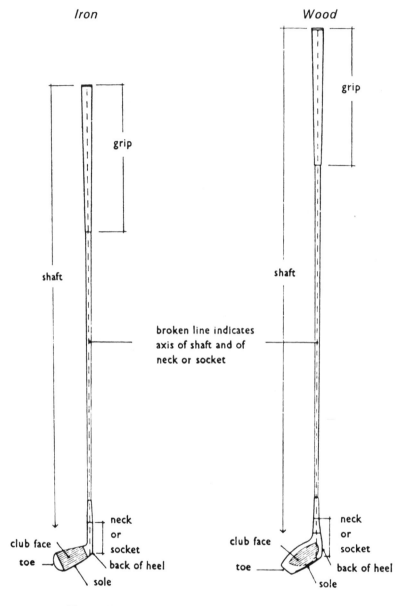

Figure A—Iron and Wood Clubs (front view)

inserted plug, shall be generally circular in cross-section and shall extend to the upper end of the grip.

The shaft shall be fixed to the clubhead at the heel (as illustrated in Figure A on page 76. The shaft may be attached directly to the clubhead or to a neck or socket of the clubhead; any neck or socket shall not be more than 5 inches (127 mm) in length measured from the top of the neck or socket to the sole. The shaft and the neck or socket shall remain in line with the heel, or with a point to right or left of the heel, when the club is soled at address. The distance between the axis of the shaft (or the neck or socket) and the back of the heel shall not exceed 0·625 inches (16 mm) in wood clubs and 0·3125 inches (8 mm) in iron clubs.

Exception for Putters: The shaft or neck or socket of a putter may be fixed at any point in the head and need not remain in line with the heel. The axis of the shaft from the top to a point not more than 5 inches (127 mm) above the sole shall diverge from the vertical by at least ten degrees in relation to the horizontal line determining length of head under Appendix IIa. The shaft in cross-section shall be generally circular or otherwise symmetrical.

d. Grip

The grip consists of that part of the shaft designed to be held by the player and any material added to it for the purpose of obtaining a firm hold. The grip shall be substantially straight and plain in form, may have flat sides, but shall not have a channel or furrow or be moulded for any part of the hands (see Figure B overleaf)."

Appendix III **Markings on Clubs** (*Def. 36*)

Rule 2-2a provides in part:
> "The golf club shall be composed of a shaft and a head, and all of the various parts shall be fixed so that the club is one unit; the club shall not be designed to be adjustable, except for weight.
> *Note: Playing characteristics not to be changed during a round—Rule 2-2b.*
> The club shall not be substantially different from the traditional and customary form and make, and shall conform with the regulations governing the design of clubs at Appendix II and the specifications for markings on clubs."

Appendix IIb provides in part:
> "Club faces shall not have any lines, dots or other markings with sharp or rough edges, or any type of finish, for the purpose of unduly influencing the movement of the ball. Markings on the face of a club shall conform with the specifications."

Sharp or rough edges of markings may be determined by a finger test. A different problem is presented, however, by the detailed Specifications for Markings on Clubs. These are manufacturing specifications. For the guidance of players and Committees, following are a layman's interpretation of some essential parts of the specifications:

In general it is required that the face of a club shall present a smooth, flat

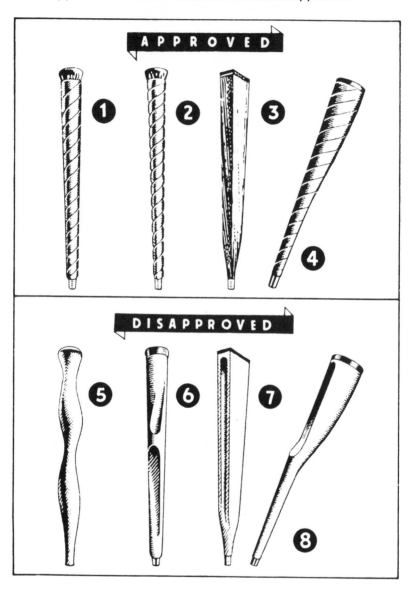

surface on which a limited percentage of the area may be depressed by markings.

When the depressed area is in the form of grooves, each groove may not be wider than ·035 inches (approximately one thirty-second of an inch) (0·9 mm), the angle between the flat surface of the club face and the side of the groove may not be less than 135 degrees. Except as provided elsewhere, the distance between grooves may not be less than three times the width of the groove.

When the depressed area is in the form of punch marks, the markings must not exceed ·075 inches (a little over one-sixteenth of an inch) (1·9 mm) in diameter.

The complete specifications are:—

Specifications

In general a definite area of the surface is reserved for scoring. All the sections contained in this specification shall refer to this particular scored area. With regard to an iron club, reasonably-sized areas of the heel and the toe shall not be scored—see illustration of "Golf Head Scorings" in Figure C on page 80. This restriction does not apply to wood clubs.

This specification is divided into three sections: Section 1 refers to golf clubs where grooves are used; Section 2 refers to golf clubs scored with punch marks; Section 3 includes a combination of groove and punch markings.

Section 1-a Wood Clubs

Wood clubs shall not have any markings on the face for the purpose of unduly influencing the movement of the ball. Where the loft or face angle exceeds 24 degrees, grooves shall be generally straight with a maximum width measured in the face plane of ·040 inches (1 mm). The depth of any groove shall not be greater than $1\frac{1}{2}$ times the width. At no place on the face shall the distance between the edges of the grooves be less than three times the width of the adjacent groove.

Section 1-b Iron Clubs

1. A series of straight grooves in the form of V's may be put in the face of the club. The side walls of the grooves shall be essentially flat and the included angle shall be equal to or greater than 90 degrees. The bisector of the angle shall be normal to the face of the club (see illustration of "Golf Head Scorings" in Figure C).

2. The width of a groove shall be generally consistent and not exceed ·035 inches (0·9 mm) along its full length. This width shall be measured in the plane of the face of the club between the two points where the planes of the groove meet the face of the club. The widths of grooves in any club face shall be generally consistent.

3. At no place on the face of the club shall the distances between edges of the grooves be less than three times the width of a groove, with the minimum distance between the edges of any two grooves being ·075 inches (1·9 mm).

4. Lines may be used to define the toe, heel and top boundaries of the scored area. Such a line must be no wider or deeper than ·040 inches (1 mm). Designs may be used to indicate the toe and heel boundaries of

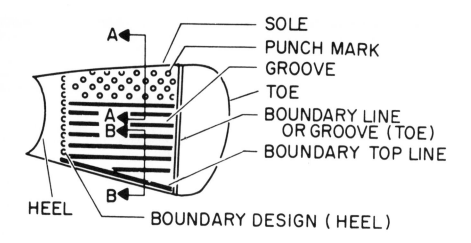

SOLE
PUNCH MARK
GROOVE
TOE
BOUNDARY LINE
    OR GROOVE (TOE)
BOUNDARY TOP LINE

HEEL

BOUNDARY DESIGN (HEEL)

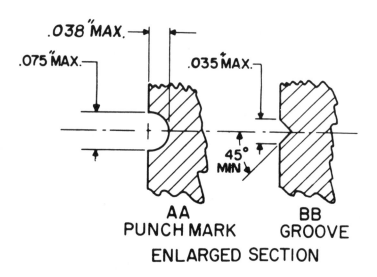

.038″ MAX.
.075″ MAX.
.035″ MAX.
45° MIN.

AA
PUNCH MARK

BB
GROOVE

ENLARGED SECTION

Figure C—Golf Head Scorings

the scored area. They must be no deeper than ·040 inches (1 mm). Designs and lines must have smooth edges and shall not be designed in any way to influence unduly the movement of the ball.

5. The scored area shall be considered as that portion of the face within boundary lines or designs. In the case where such lines or designs do not exist, the scored area shall be that portion between the extremities of the grooves.

6. The centre or intended impact centre of the face may be indicated by a design which shall fit within the boundary of a square whose sides are 0·375 inches (9·5 mm) in length. Such a marking shall not in anyway be designed to influence unduly the movement of the ball.

7. The face of the club shall be smooth and flat over the full surface. No sharp edges or lips due to die impression of any type will be permitted. For decorative purposes only, it is permissible to sandblast the scored area not to exceed a roughness of 180 micro inches (4·6 microns), with 15% tolerance. The relative roughness shall be determined in accordance with British standards for surface texture. The direction of measurement shall be parallel to the grooves.

The above conditions for smoothness apply also to Sections 2 and 3.

Section 2

Punch marks may be used in the place of grooves. The area of such a mark, in the plane of the face, may not exceed ·0044 square inches (2·8 sq mm). A mark may not be closer to an adjacent mark than 0·168 inches (4·3 mm) measured from centre to centre. The depth of a mark may not be greater than ·038 inches (1 mm) with centre line normal to the face. Punch marks must be evenly distributed throughout the scored area.

Section 3

In the event punch marks in combination with grooves are used within the scored area, groove specifications govern as in Section 1 if grooves are adjacent. Punch mark specifications govern if punch marks are adjacent. At no place may a punch mark be closer to a groove measured from centre to centre than 0·168 inches (4·3 mm).

Handicaps in General Use

MATCH PLAY

Singles 3/4ths of the difference between the full handicaps of the two players.

Foursomes 3/8ths of the difference between the aggregate handicaps on either side.

Four-ball Back marker to concede strokes to other three players based on 3/4ths of the difference between the full handicaps.
Strokes to be taken according to the Stroke Table.

BOGEY OR PAR COMPETITIONS

Singles 3/4ths of full handicap.

Foursomes 3/8ths of the aggregate handicaps of the partners.

Four-ball Each partner receives 3/4ths of full handicap.
Strokes to be taken according to the Stroke Table.

STROKE PLAY

Singles Full handicap.

Foursomes 1/2 of aggregate handicaps of the partners.

Four-ball Each partner receives 3/4ths of the full handicap and strokes to be taken according to the Stroke Table.

STABLEFORD COMPETITIONS

Singles 7/8ths of full handicap.

Foursomes 7/16ths of aggregate handicaps of the partners.

Four-ball Each partner receives 7/8ths of full handicap.
Strokes to be taken according to the Stroke Table and not added to the points scored.

Note 1. *Half Strokes*
Half strokes or over to be counted as one; smaller fractions to be disregarded.

2. *Handicaps*
Detailed methods of handicapping are not covered by the Rules of Golf and must be laid down by the Committee in the Conditions of the Competition (Rule 36-1).

3. *36-hole competitions*
In handicap competitions over 36 holes, strokes should be given or taken in accordance with the 18 hole Stroke Table unless the Committee introduces a special Stroke Table.

4. *Sudden-death play-off*
When extra holes are played in handicap competitions, strokes should be taken in accordance with the Stroke Table.

Rules of Amateur Status

(Effective from 1st January 1976)
as approved by the Royal and Ancient Golf Club of St. Andrews

Any person who considers that any action he is proposing to take might endanger his Amateur Status should submit particulars to the Committee for consideration.

DEFINITION OF AN AMATEUR GOLFER
An amateur golfer is one who plays the game solely as a non-remunerative or non-profit-making sport.

RULE 1

FORFEITURE OF AMATEUR STATUS AT ANY AGE
The following are examples of acts at any age which violate the Definition of an Amateur Golfer and cause forfeiture of amateur status:

1. Professionalism.
a. Receiving payment or compensation for serving as a professional golfer or a teaching or playing assistant to a professional golfer.
b. Taking any action for the purpose of becoming a professional golfer.

2. Playing for Prize Money. Playing for prize money or its equivalent in a match, tournament or exhibition.

3. Instruction. Receiving payment or compensation for giving instruction in playing golf, either orally, in writing, by pictures or by other demonstrations, to either individuals or groups.
Exception:
Teachers of physical training or other subjects whose duties include instruction in games to pupils of a recognised educational establishment.

4. Prizes and Testimonials. Acceptance of a prize or testimonial of the following character (this applies to total prizes received for any event or series of events in any one tournament or exhibition, including hole-in-one or other events in which golf skill is a factor):

(i) In Great Britain and Ireland, of retail value exceeding £100, elsewhere, of retail value exceeding $250 U.S. or the equivalent, or such lesser figure as may be decided by the Governing Body of Golf in any country; or

(ii) Of a nature which is the equivalent of money or makes it readily convertible into money.

Exceptions:
1. Prizes of only symbolic value (such as metal trophies).
2. More than one testimonial award may be accepted from different donors even though their total retail value exceeds £100 or $250 U.S., provided they are not presented so as to evade such value limit for a single award. (Testimonial awards relate to notable performances or contributions to golf, as distinguished from tournament prizes).

5. Lending Name or Likeness. Because of golf skill or golf reputation, receiving or contracting to receive payment, compensation or personal benefit, directly or indirectly, for allowing one's name or likeness to be used in any way for the advertisement or sale of anything, whether or not used in or appertaining to golf.

Note: *An advertisement may contain a player's name or likeness when it is customary to the business of such a player and contains no reference to the game of golf.*

6. Personal Appearance. Because of golf skill or golf reputation, receiving payment or compensation, directly or indirectly, for a personal appearance.
Exception:
Actual expenses in connection with personal appearances may be paid or reimbursed provided no golf competition or exhibition is involved.

7. Writing. Because of golf skill, receiving or contracting to receive payment or compensation, directly or indirectly, for writing golf articles or books or for allowing one's name to be advertised or published as the author of golf articles or books of which he is not actually the author. (See Rule 1-3).

8. Sale of Golf Merchandise. Because of golf skill or golf reputation, receiving payment or compensation, directly or indirectly, for selling or promoting the sale of golf merchandise, at either wholesale or retail. (The term "golf merchandise" does not include clothing or shoes).

9. Golf Equipment. Accepting golf balls, clubs, golf merchandise, golf clothing or golf shoes from anyone dealing in such merchandise without payment of current market price.

10. Membership and Privileges. Because of golf skill or golf reputation, accepting membership or privileges in a club or at a golf course without full payment for the class of membership or privileges involved unless such membership or privileges have been awarded as purely and deservedly honorary and in recognition of an outstanding performance or contribution to golf.

11. Expenses. Accepting expenses, in money or otherwise, from any source to engage in a golf competition or exhibition.
Exceptions:
A player may receive a reasonable amount of expenses as follows:
1. From a member of the family or legal guardian;
or
2. As a player in a golf competition or exhibition limited exclusively to players who have not reached their 18th birthday;
or
3. As a representative of his country, county, club or similar body, in team matches, or as a representative of his country taking part in a National Championship abroad immediately preceding or following directly upon an international team match, where such expenses are paid by the body he represents, or by the body controlling golf in the territory he is visiting:
or
4. As an individual nominated by a National or County (or equivalent) Union to engage in a National or County event, at home or abroad,

subject to the agreement of the National Union and the National Union of the Country staging the event, *provided* the individual has not reached the age of 22 (or such age, not exceeding 25, as may be determined by the Governing Body of Golf in the country concerned) and *provided* the expenses shall only be paid by the National or County (or equivalent) Union nominating the player.

5. As a player invited for reasons unrelated to golf skill, e.g. celebrities, business associates, etc., to take part in golfing events.

Note 1: Business Expenses. *It is permissible to play in a golf competition while on a business trip with expenses paid provided that the golf part of the expenses is borne personally and is not charged to business. Further, the business involved must be actual and substantial, and not merely a subterfuge for legitimising expenses when the primary purpose is a golf competition.*

Note 2: Private Transport. *Acceptance of private transport furnished or arranged for by a tournament sponsor, directly or indirectly, as an inducement for a player to engage in a golf competition or exhibition shall be considered accepting expenses under Rule 1-11.*

12. Scholarships. Because of golf skill or golf reputation, accepting the benefits of a scholarship or any other consideration as an inducement to be a student in an educational establishment.

13. Conduct Detrimental to Golf. Any conduct, including activities in connection with golf gambling, which is considered detrimental to the best interests of the game.

RULE 2

PROCEDURE FOR ENFORCEMENT AND REINSTATEMENT

1. Decision on Violation. Whenever information of a possible violation of the Definition of an Amateur Golfer by a player claiming to be an amateur shall come to the attention of the Executive Committee of the Governing Body, the Committee, after such investigation as it may deem desirable, shall decide whether a violation has occurred. Each case shall be considered on its merits. The decision of the Committee shall be final.

2. Enforcement. Upon a decision that a player has violated the Definition of an Amateur Golfer, the Committee may declare the amateur status of the player forfeited or require the player to refrain or desist from specified actions as a condition of retaining his amateur status.

The Committee shall notify the player, if possible, and may notify any interested golf association of any action taken under this paragraph.

3. Reinstatement. The Committee shall have sole power to reinstate a player to amateur status or to deny reinstatement.

Each application for reinstatement shall be decided on its merits.

In considering an application for reinstatement, the Committee shall normally be guided by the following principles:

a. Probation.

The professional holds an advantage over the amateur by reason of having devoted himself to the game as his profession; other persons violating the Rules of Amateur Status also obtain advantages not available to the amateur. They do not necessarily lose such advantage merely by deciding to cease violating the Rules.

Therefore, an applicant for reinstatement to Amateur Status shall undergo probation as prescribed by the Committee.

Probation shall start from the date of the player's last violation of the Definition of an Amateur Golfer unless the Committee decides that it shall start from the date when the player's last violation became known to the Committee.

b. Probationary Period.

The period of probation shall normally be related to the period the player was in violation. However, no applicant shall normally be eligible for reinstatement until he has conducted himself in accordance with the Definition of an Amateur Golfer for a probationary period of at least two consecutive years. The Committee, however, reserves the right to extend or to shorten such a period. A longer period will normally be required of applicants who have been in violation more than five years.

Players of national prominence who have been in violation for more than five years shall not normally be eligible for reinstatement.

c. One Reinstatement.

A player shall not normally be reinstated more than once.

d. Status during Probation.

During probation an applicant for reinstatement shall conform with the Definition of an Amateur Golfer.

He shall not be eligible to enter competitions as an amateur. He may, however, enter competitions solely among members of a Club of which he is a member, subject to the approval of the Club, but he may not represent such Club against other Clubs.

Forms of Application for Countries under the jurisdiction of the Royal and Ancient Golf Club

Each application for reinstatement in England, Scotland, Ireland and Wales shall be submitted on the approved form to the County Union, District Association or Provincial Branch of the area where the Applicant wishes to play as an Amateur. The body concerned shall, after making all necessary enquiries, forward it through the National Union and the Professional Golfers' Association, with comments endorsed thereon, to the Royal and Ancient Golf Club of St. Andrews. Forms of application for reinstatement may be obtained from the Royal and Ancient Golf Club or from the National or County Unions. The Application shall include such information as the Royal and Ancient Golf Club may require from time to time and it shall be signed and certified by the Applicant.

Any application made elsewhere in countries, under the jurisdiction of the Royal and Ancient Golf Club of St. Andrews which is doubtful or which is not covered by the above regulations may be submitted to the Royal and Ancient Golf Club through the Governing Body of Golf in that country.

The decision of the Royal and Ancient Golf Club on an application shall be final.

INDEX

mulligan, 129

nap, 77, 129
Nassau bet, 115, 129
national associations, 93
New Zealand Open Championship, 26
niblicks, 129
no man's land, 36

Oakmont course, 67
observer, 129, 135-136
obstructions, 58-63, 67, 88, 92, 129, 136, 157, 159, 166
odd, playing the, 129
Old Man Par, 107
one-piece golf ball, 122
one-stroke penalty, 32-33, 73
on the green, 76-85, 103-105
order and times of starting, 165, 167
order of play, 145-146, 171, 173
ordinary water hazard, 43-44
out of bounds ball, 17-18, 35-36, 54, 74, 88, 90, 129, 136, 155-156
out of bounds, standing, 36, 155
out of play
    ball, 90
    clubs, 14, 140
outside agencies, interfering with play, 45-50, 52, 90, 123, 129, 136, 152-153
overhanging ball, 79-80, 163

Palmer, Arnold, 6-7, 35, 71
par, 107, 129
par competitions, 107-108, 169-170
partner, 129, 136
'paying' a stroke, 33-34
penalty, 32-44, 130, 136, 140
    artificial aids, 27
    breaking a rule, 32-33, 75, 140
    cheating, 32
    drop in wrong place, 155
    excess clubs, 14
    grounding club, 65, 71
    hitting objects with ball, 32, 47, 50, 78, 81
    infringement of rule, 111
    lifting and dropping, 32, 35, 36, 44
    marking the line, 23
    moving immovable obstruction, 62
    moving the ball, 32-33, 40, 50, 59
    not replacing ball, 46
    playing out of turn, 108
    playing outside teeing ground, 90
    practice stroke, 25-26
    removing loose impediments, 75
    shanking, 32
    stealing the honour, 17
    stroke-and-distance rule, 18
    touching ball in play, 15, 34
    unplayable ball, 24, 34, 56
    waiving a rule, 17
    wrong ball, 32, 42-43

physical danger, right to take evasive action, 93, 123-124
'pin,' 89
pin high, 130
pitch, 130
pitch marks, repairing, 76-77, 92, 104
placing a ball, 28, 34, 42, 52, 84-85, 89, 92, 150
player, 167-168
    fast, 102-103
    slow, 68, 99-100, 102
playing ball as it lies, 17, 23-25, 38, 146
playing out of turn, 16, 108, 144, 147, 148, 164, 171
position, when another player is taking a shot, 98-99
pot bunkers, 67
practice ground, 166
practice stance, 74
practice strokes, 25-26, 92, 131, 137, 141-142
practice swings, 25-26, 92, 97-98, 133, 142
precedent, solving legal problems by, 123
predicaments, escape clause for, 17-18
'press,' 115, 130
priority through the course, 102-103, 132
prizes, 93-94, 114
pro-ams, 112-113
probation, for violations, 185-186
provisional ball, 36-37, 43, 90, 92, 120, 133, 143-144, 156
pull, 130
Pung, Jackie, 87
push, 130
pushing the ball, 22
putter, 138
putter club, 14
putting, 76-85, 130, 162
    croquet putting, 28, 79
putting ball into play, 52
putting green, 136, 162-165

queries, referred for arbitration, 16, 117

'rabbit,' 110
rangefinders, 27
'reading the nap,' 77
rebounding ball, 47, 52, 81
reckoning of holes, terms, 137
referee, responsibility, 124, 130, 136, 143
refusal to comply with rules, 168
reinstatement to amateur status, 185
relief from interference, 29, 58-63, 68, 157-158
replacing a ball, 28, 92, 108, 111
replacing a club, 12-14, 92, 122, 139
replaying a stroke, 71
reptiles, interfering with play, 56
re-putt, right to, 111
rights and duties, 86-95
rolling ball, after being dropped, 54-56, 149, 159
rolling the ball, 89
rough, 89

round
  beginning, 16
  stipulated, 137
Round Robins, 112, 130
Royal and Ancient Golf Club of St. Andrews, 16, 27, 93, 117-124
rubber core ball, 130
'rub of the green,' 30, 130, 136, 152
rule book, how to consult, 89-90
rules
  as allies, 9, 33-34, 90-93
  dual system for stroke- and match-play, 19-20
  earliest code, 6
  foundation of golf law, 17
  how to learn, 73
  knowing and using, 88-89
  local, 12, 36, 43-44, 57, 88-89, 128, 166, 174-175
  penalty for breaking, 32-33
  rule of equity, 10, 30, 86, 121, 124, 143
  rule of the road, 102-103
  rules vs conventions, 16
  waiving of, 16-17, 140, 166
  winter rules, 88, 131
Rules of Amateur Status, 183-186
Rules of Golf, 16, 89, 96, 117-124, 132-187
Rules of Golf Committee, 15, 25, 27, 28, 34, 58, 71, 73, 75, 117-124
Rules of Play, 138-181
rut irons, 17

sand shots, 65, 67
sand, smoothing, 68-72
sand wedges, 14, 130
scoring, in stroke-play, 168-169
Scotch Foursomes, 108
scrapes, from burrowing animals, 56-58, 68, 84, 90, 93, 158
scraping the ball, 22
scratch, 130
searching for lost ball, 37-38, 65-66, 92, 103, 128, 133-134, 155-159
semi-rough, 89
sixteen club set, 14
shaft, design, 175-177
shank, 32, 130
sharing clubs, 14, 139
'side,' playing as a, 110, 137
single match, 137
slice, 130
slow play, 68, 99-100, 102
Snead, Sam, 79, 86
socket, 130
solid golf ball, 122
specialized clubs, 17
spike marks, 77, 104
spirit levels, 27
split ball, 122
spooning the ball, 22
spoons, 131
Stableford competitions, 107-108, 131, 169-170

stance, 24-25, 131, 137, 146
starting, order and times of, 165, 167
stationary ball, moved, 46-47, 50
stealing the honour, 16-17
stepping on the ball, 40-42
'stick,' 89
Still, Ken, 110
stipulated round, 137
striking the ball, 147
stroke, 65
stroke-and-distance rule, 17-18, 34-38, 43-44, 68, 74
stroke, cancelling, 46
stroke-play, 19-20, 89, 106-108, 131, 141
  four-ball stroke-play, 172-174
strokes, practice, 25-26, 92, 131, 137, 141-142
suspending play, 92, 123
swings, practice, 25-26, 92, 97-98, 133, 142

'taking the honour,' 16
Taylor, J.H., 26
tee, 14, 17, 90, 131, 137
  ball falling off, 15, 90, 145
teeing ground, 14-15, 18, 52, 98, 131
  playing outside of, 15, 90, 137, 144-145
testing surface condition, 67, 74, 75, 77-78, 163
Texas wedge, 131
'thinning' the shot, 75
third tee stroke, in a drive, 36
three-ball match-play, 109, 131, 137, 170-172
three-man golf variations, 109-110
threesomes, 109, 131, 137, 145-146
'through the green,' 21-34, 89, 131, 137
ties, decision of, 165
'tiger,' 110, 113
time and order of starting, 165, 167
'to play' holes, 137
top shot, 131
touching a ball in play, 15
touching the line, 78
trap, 64, 89, 131
Trevino, Lee, 27
two club-lengths measurement, 15, 34, 54, 56, 62, 73
'two golf balls a side' bet, 115
two-stroke penalty, 15, 23, 25, 26, 32, 43, 47, 54, 56, 62, 65, 78, 81, 108

undue delay, 12, 28, 76, 98-100, 104-105, 168
unfit for play ball, 28, 92, 122, 154-155
United States Golf Association, 16, 71, 93, 114, 117
unplayable ball, 17, 24, 30, 34-35, 56, 68, 155-156
unplayable course, 166
unplayable lie, 33-35

Vardon, Harry, 26

wagers, 106-116
waggle, 131